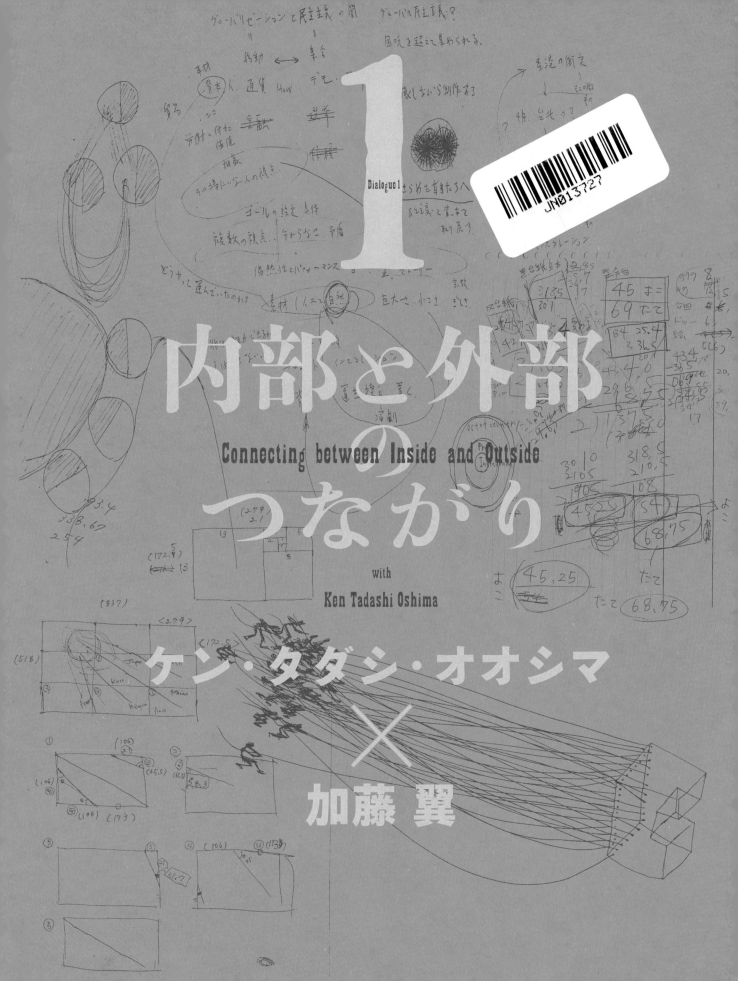

内部と外部のつながり

Connecting between Inside and Outside

with
Ken Tadashi Oshima

ケン・タダシ・オオシマ ✕ 加藤 翼

Dialogue 1

1

ケン・タダシ・オオシマ

ワシントン大学建築学部教授。専門は建築史、建築論および建築デザイン。1965年アメリカ・コロラド州生まれ。国際建築史家協会（SAH）会長（2016〜2018 年）。主な著書に『Architecturalized Asia』（2013年）、『International Architecture in Interwar Japan』（2009年）、『Arata Isozaki』（2009年）、キュレーションした展示に「日本を超えた日本建築-Beyond Japan-」（谷口吉郎・吉生記念 金沢建築館、2020年）、「Tectonic Visions Between Land and Sea: Works of Kiyonori Kikutake」（ハーバード大学デザイン大学院、2012年）、「グローバル・エンズ：始まりに向けて」（TOTO ギャラリー・間、2010〜11年）など。建築誌『Architecture and Urbanism（a+u）』の編集・執筆を 10 年以上にわたって務め、国際的な文脈における日本の建築と都市計画に関する執筆・講演を数多く行なっている。

Ken Tadashi Oshima   Professor at the University of Washington, Department of Architecture (architectural history, theory, and design). Born in 1965 in Colorado, USA, he served as President of the Society of Architectural Historians (SAH) from 2016 to 2018 and was an editor and contributor to *Architecture and Urbanism (a+u)* for more than ten years. His publications include *Architecturalized Asia* (2013), *International Architecture in Interwar Japan* (2009), and *Arata Isozaki* (2009). He curated exhibitions such as *Beyond Japan* (Yoshiro and Yoshio Taniguchi Museum of Architecture, Kanazawa, 2020), *Tectonic Visions Between Land and Sea: Works of Kiyonori Kikutake* (Harvard GSD, 2012), *GLOBAL ENDS: towards the beginning* (TOTO GALLERY・MA, 2010-11). Dr. Oshima has been writing and giving lectures extensively on architecture and urban planning in Japan in its international context.

加藤翼　縄張りと島

Tsubasa Kato: Turf and Perimeter

目 次

Contents

加藤翼
Tsubasa Kato

縄張りと島のその先へ

堀　元彰

東京オペラシティ アートギャラリー チーフ・キュレーター

1.

　8年前の2013年7月22日朝、JR南浦和駅で電車から降りようとした乗客の女性が、電車とホームの隙間に落ちて身動きができなくなった。このとき、車内やホームに居合わせた40人ほどが車両を押して隙間を広げ、女性を無事救出した。この出来事は国内のテレビや新聞でも報道されたほか、CNNやSNSを通じて世界中に拡散し、大きな反響を呼んだ。

　偶然その場に居合わせた見ず知らずの人々が、率先して力を合わせて、重さ32トンの車両を押して救助にあたる光景は、人々の相互扶助の心、連帯意識の重要性をあらためて実感させるものだった。たとえ一人ひとりの力は微力であっても、多くの人が心をひとつにして協力すれば、不可能に思えることも可能となる。長い歴史のなかでさまざまな試練に遭遇し、その都度結束して困難や危機を乗り越えてきた人類の歴史をも彷彿させる出来事だったといえよう。

　当時このニュースをネットで目にしたとき、ふと思い浮かんだのが加藤翼の「引き倒し・引き興し」だった。2007年の五美大展の会場で初めて彼の作品（おそらく《g.g.g.02》だったように思う）をみて、重量のある構造体を数人がかりで必死に引き倒そうと奮闘する映像に思わず引き込まれ、しばし見入ってしまったのを覚えている。共通の目的をなし遂げるため一致団結するさまは、たとえそれがどんなに

g.g.g. 02 2007

1.

Eight years ago, on the morning of July 23, 2013, a woman detraining at Minami Urawa station misstepped and fell into the crevice between the train and the platform. She was unable to move. Forty-some people from the train and waiting on the platform spontaneously teamed up to push against the train, creating enough space so that the woman could be rescued. This near-disaster was covered not only by domestic television news and print media in Japan, but also on CNN and social media, thus creating waves around the world.

Witnessing so many strangers, with nothing in common other than that they happened to be in the same place at the same time, taking it upon themselves to pool their strength to move a 32-ton train car to save another stranger reaffirmed for me the urgent importance of a spirit of mutual aid and solidarity. Alone, each person's strength may be trivial. But when many put their hearts together and work as one, the impossible becomes possible. The history of the human race is a history of trials, of people binding together to overcome difficulties and crises. The episode in Minami Urawa was also a reminder of that.

When I saw this story on the internet, Tsubasa Kato's "pull and raise" and "pull and topple" projects immediately popped into mind. I first saw his work in 2007, at the annual Joint Graduation Exhibition of 5 Art Universities in Tokyo. It was presumably his work *g.g.g. 02* that I saw, but I remember being enrapt by a video showing multiple people struggling desperately to pull down a large and heavy mass. When people come together to achieve a common goal, no matter how silly or ridiculous that goal might seem, the sight is an inspiration to anyone who witnesses it.

The international reaction to the Minami Urawa story, with its images of passengers joining railway staff to push with all their might against the train, affirms this. Since 2011, Kato has expanded his field of ideas and activity beyond Japan, again demonstrating the transcultural and transnational universality of projects involving collaborative human action directed toward a common goal.

The Lighthouses – 11.3 PROJECT (2011), which Kato created in the wake of the Tohoku Earthquake and Tsunami, likewise demonstrates the unmatchable power and potential of human solidarity. Previously, Kato had served as a volunteer cleaning up debris and delivering

ナンセンスで他愛もない目的であろうと、みる者の心を強く突き動かすものなのだろう。

　車体を懸命に押そうとする駅員に次々と加勢した乗客たちの行動やそのニュースに対する世界中からの反響も、そのことを裏づけるものに違いない。2011年以降加藤は作品の着想や実施の場所を海外に広げているが、ひとつの目標に向かって協働するプロジェクトは、文化や国民性の相違を超えて、万国共通のなかば普遍的な原則として受け入れられている。

　東日本大震災が発生した2011年に加藤が制作した《**The Lighthouses-11.3 PROJECT**》(2011) も、人々の団結のかけがえのない力と可能性を教えてくれる作品だ。これに先立ち加藤は、福島県いわき市で避難所への生活物資の支給や炊き出し、瓦礫の撤去作業にボランティアとして参加するかたわら、家を失った家主たちから大量の木材の提供を受けた。プロジェクトは、未曾有の大災害が起こった3月11日を逆にした11月3日の文化の日に行われた。加藤の呼びかけに応じた約500人の人々が集まり、津波で壊された家々の木材によって、灯台のイメージに組みあげられた構造体をロープで引き起こした。さらに、このプロジェクトの構想が契機になり、震災からの復興を目指す地区のお祭りの開催へと発展した。

2.

　東日本大震災は作品制作や美術それ自体に対するアーティストの意識や姿勢に少なからぬ影響をもたらしたが、なかでも加藤翼は最も大きな影響を受けたアーティストの一人といえるだろう。震災発生時、加藤は大阪城公園での《**H.H.H.A.**(ホーム, ホテルズ, 秀吉, アウェイ)》の引き倒しを翌日に控え、大阪に滞在していた。2010年度「おおさかカンヴァス推進事業」の一環で、中央公会堂前で行った1回目

and distributing food and other provisions at evacuation sites in Iwaki, in southeastern Fukushima. The lumber he used for the project was given to him by people whose homes had been destroyed by the tsunami. The event was held on Culture Day, a national holiday celebrated on November 3–which is to say, on 11.3, an inversion of 3.11, March 11, the date of that unforgettable catastrophe. With approximately 500 people in attendance, the participants pulled on ropes to raise a lighthouse built of lumber from homes destroyed by the tsunami. What started out as an art project transformed into a festival, honoring the hopes of all those wishing for a speedy recovery from the disaster.

2.

The 2011 Earthquake and Tsunami had a significant impact on artists' consciousness, the way they position themselves, and how they make work, as it did on the art world at large. Kato is a prime example. At the time of the earthquake, he was staying in Osaka, preparing for a "pull and topple" project in Osaka Castle Park titled *H.H.H.A. (Home, Hotels, Hideyoshi, Away)*, to be conducted the next day. As part of the Osaka Canvas Project, Kato had previously executed a performance in front of the Osaka City Central Public Hall in 2010, and this was to be its sequel. However, shocked by videos of homes swept away by the tsunami, Kato changed his plans. He decided to have people pulling from both sides to slowly raise the structure instead. Soon after that, he conducted a third "pull and raise" event in Osaka at the Expo '70 Commemorative Park , which in turn led to the aforementioned *The Lighthouses – 11.3 PROJECT*.

Two years later, in 2013, Kato went to the United States. Traveling around by car, he looked for abandoned cars and buildings to pull up and over with ropes. Collectively known as the *Abandon* series, these performances alighted upon bankrupt Detroit, the toxic Salton Sea, and other sites that reflected the straits and strains that led to Donald Trump winning the 2016 presidential election.

Kato's first visit to Standing Rock Reservation was during this road trip across the United States. Perceiving a resonance between Japanese displaced by the tsunami and the nuclear meltdowns and Native Americans forcibly confined to reservations, Kato carried out *Boarding School* (2013), *Black Snake* (2017), and *Underground Orchestra* (2017) at Standing Rock in collaboration with members of the local Sioux tribe.

It is thus that, since the 2011 disaster, Kato's engagement with fundamental social and political issues has extended far beyond *The Lighthouses – 11.3 PROJECT*. As Kato was born in 1984, it is easy to imagine that the world to him is not a place governed by peace and mindless stability, but rather a brittle and unstable environment cut through with risks and crises. We live in an age that is not only menaced by terrorism– especially since the 9/11 attacks in the United States in 2001–but also earthquakes, floods, and other largescale natural catastrophes that seem to now befall the world yearly. Local communities, confronted with

に続く、2回目の引き倒しになる予定だった。だが、津波が家屋をなぎ倒すニュースの映像を目の当たりにして、思い悩んだ末にパフォーマンスの中止を決定。その翌日、引き倒すのではなく、両方向から引っ張りながら、ゆっくりと引き起こすプランに変更し、プロジェクトを実施した。その後、万博記念公園で3回目の引き興しを行い、これが発展して、先述の《**The Lighthouses-11.3 PROJECT**》の結実につながっている。

　震災から2年後の2013年、加藤はアメリカに渡り、車で各地を訪れ、打ち捨てられた車、家などをみつけては、ロープをかけて引っ張ることを試みる。《**Abandon**》(2013)と題されたこのシリーズには、財政破綻したデトロイトや環境悪化が進むソルトン湖など、3年後の2016年のアメリカ大統領選挙で浮き彫りになるアメリカ社会の疲弊や歪みがいみじくも映し出されている。

Abandon (Black Hills) 2013

スー族のスタンディングロック居留地を初めて訪れたのも、このアメリカ一周のときだった。居留地に強制移住させられたネイティブアメリカンの歴史に、津波や原発事故のため移住を余儀なくされた被災者たちのいまを重ね合わせ、《**Board-ing School**》(2013)、《**Black Snake**》(2017)、《**Underground Orchestra**》(2017)などの作品を制作している。

　震災以後、加藤翼が世に問うてきた作品は、《**The Lighthouses-11.3 PROJ-ECT**》に限らず、その根底において当時の社会や政治の動向と密接に関わっている。1984年生まれの加藤にとって、世界というものは平穏無事で安全なものなどではなく、つねにさまざまな脅威や危機に晒される脆く不安定なものなのかもしれない。アメリカ同時多発テロ以後、世界各地で頻発するテロの脅威、東日本大震災をはじめ、毎年のように発生する地震や豪雨などの大規模な自然災害が世界に襲いかかる時代である。加藤の作品が、自然災害、都市開発、環境破壊などで地域のコミュニティが解体の危機に瀕するなか、人々が自発的に参画し、一体となって何かを実践することの意義を提示するのは、脅威が繰り返されるこうした時代と、それに対する鋭敏な感性が背景にあるからに違いない。

mortal threats to their very being from natural disasters, urban development, and environmental crises, are continually forced to devise their own responses and collective actions in order to survive. Paradigmatic of our age, Kato's work draws on that very tension.

Boarding School 2013

Black Snake 2017

3.
For his Tokyo Opera City Art Gallery exhibition—his first solo show at a museum—Kato has chosen the unique title of *Turf and Perimeter*. In Japanese, it's *Nawabari to Shima*. The first term, "nawabari," is often used to describe the arbitrary and monopolistic control of an area by gangs or yakuza. Since "shima," literally "island," can be used as a colloquial name for the same, the title of Kato's exhibition is, in a sense, redundant. However, "nawabari" is also used to indicate a specific individual or group's range of action or field of specialization. Within animal ecology, the term refers to a controlled territory into which competing individuals or groups are prohibited from entering. The concept of "personal space" within behavioral psychology might also be understood as a kind of "nawabari."

Sometimes, groups with conflicting beliefs or values end up warring over territory. Kato's *Underground Orchestra* (2017), shot in Standing Rock, is a good example. In that work, small animals have been driven from their homes (their turf) by humans battling over rights and the environment. Their presence is translated into the chiming of bells hung at the openings of their abodes, the sound echoing peacefully across a plain that stretches as far as the eye can see. It is a work that draws attention to the importance of setting aside political differences—in this case, the fight over the pipeline—and finding ways to coexist with nature and attend to those who are vulnerable to the vagaries of human hubris.

Underground Orchestra 2017

3.

　美術館での初個展のタイトルとして、加藤は「縄張りと島」というユニークなフレーズを選んだ。「縄張り」は、ギャングやヤクザなどが独占的、恣意的に支配する勢力範囲の呼称としてよく知られ、「島（シマ）」はその隠語だから、「縄張りと島」は同語反復になっている。なお、縄張りは転じて、特定の個人や集団の行動範囲や専門領域を広く指す言葉としても使われる。また、動物生態学の分野でも、競争関係にある個体や集団を侵入させないよう占有する一定の範囲や領分を縄張りと呼ぶほか、行動心理学でいう「パーソナル・スペース」も縄張りの一種といえる。

　信条や価値観を異にする２つの集団の縄張り争いが及ぼす影響を作品化したのが、スー族のスタンディングロック居留地で撮影された《**Underground Orchestra**》(2017) である。利権や環境をめぐる人間の争いのかげで、棲家（＝縄張り）を追われた小動物の存在が巣穴の入口に仕掛けられた鈴の音に変換され、見渡すかぎりの草原に静かに響きわたる。パイプラインの建設賛成・反対という立場を超えて、人間の傲慢さやその犠牲になる弱者への眼差し、自然との共生の重要性が提示されている。

　また、同じく 2017 年に制作された《**Woodstock 2017**》では、高架下で４人の白人男性がアメリカ国歌を演奏するが、各奏者は互いに縄で拘束されている。そのため、1人が自由に演奏しようとすると、他のメンバーの妨げになり、演奏が成り立たない。この年、第 45 代大統領に就任したドナルド・トランプは、人種差別に抗議して国歌斉唱時に起立を拒否するアスリートたちを激しく糾弾し、アメリカ社会の分断に拍車をかけた。不協和音を奏でる演奏は、現代社会の分断と対立を強

Woodstock 2017 2017

In *Woodstock 2017* (2017), four White guys are shown attempting to play the American national anthem while tied to one another with ropes. Whenever any of them try to play their instruments as he wishes, it interferes with the others playing theirs, making a successful performance impossible. That same year, Donald Trump, recently elected as the 45th President of the United States, exacerbated divisions within American society by denouncing athletes who refused to stand for the American national anthem in protest against racial injustice. Not only did the dissonant performance in Kato's *Woodstock 2017* reflect divisions and antagonisms within contemporary society, but the performers' struggle to play despite their restraints also raises important questions about the nature of freedom today.

In *2679* (2019), three people attempt to perform *Kimigayo*, the Japanese national anthem, playing a

く意識させるとともに、不自由に耐えながら演奏を続ける彼らの姿からは、自由というものの本質がまざまざと浮かび上がってくるようだ。

　三味線、琴、太鼓の３人の演奏者が「君が代」を演奏する《2679》(2019) も、《**Woodstock 2017**》と同じ「拘束の演奏」で、個人の自由の境界線、パーソナル・スペースと呼ばれる縄張りを顕在化させる。なお、とくに明示されていないが、３人の奏者がみな両親のいずれかが外国出身者だということも、作品にもうひとつのレイヤーを与えている。

2679　2019

「縄張り」の語源は文字どおり、土地に縄を張って境界線を定め、また、そこが特別な区画であると示したことに由来する。このように縄張りの縄は、排他性や独占性を意味するためにもちいられた。それに対して、加藤が作品にもちいる縄は人々の協働を促すツールであり、そのシンボルといってもよいだろう。

4.
　恣意的な縄張りをめぐる加藤の眼差しはマレーシア、ベトナム、香港など、アジアにも向けられている。《**Break it Before it's Broken**》(2015) は、フィリピンのミンダナオ島から紛争を逃れ、マレーシアで無国籍者として暮らす人々と行った「引き倒し・引き興し」の一部始終を記録する。権力や暴力により幾度となく移住を強いられてきた彼らは、縄張り争いの犠牲者といえるだろう。休憩中の監視の目を盗んでゲリラ的に行われた《**Guerrilla Waves**》(2017) に登場するボートは、ベ

Guerrilla Waves　2017

トナム戦争末期以降国外逃亡の象徴となった。ベトナム政府はいまもなお、公共空間における集会や表現の自由を制限するが、この作品は、ベトナム政府の縄張りへの侵犯行為を通じて、自由が許されない現状を痛烈に告発する。
　また、《**言葉が通じない**》(2014) では、加藤と対馬で出会った韓国人男性が協力し

shamisen, a koto, and a taiko drum. Like *Woodstock 2017*, the performance is physically restrained and highlights the limits of personal freedom and personal space–that is, it highlights issues pertaining to turf and territory. Though this is not readily apparent from watching the video, each performer has one parent who is not Japanese, adding another layer of symbolism to the work.

As the word in Japanese suggests, "nawabari" (literally, "rope-stretching") originates from the practice of demarcating boundaries with a rope and the special space created thereby. The "rope" of "nawabari" thus signifies the exclusion of others and the creation of a monopoly for oneself. In contrast, the rope used by Kato in his performances is a tool that brings people together and a symbol of collectivity.

4.
Kato's attention to arbitrarily imposed territory also extends to Malaysia, Vietnam, Hong Kong, and other Asian locales. In the form of a "pull and raise/topple" performance, *Break it Before it's Broken* (2015), for example, documents the fate of peoples driven by war from their home in Mindanao, Philippines, and settling in Malaysia as stateless people. Forced as they were to relocate repeatedly because of abuses of power and violence, one could call these migrants victims of "nawabari" struggles. The boat used in *Guerilla Waves* (2017), a performance conducted surreptitiously while security guards were on break, is likewise a symbol of refugees, this time from the Vietnam War. Even today, the Vietnamese government restricts rights of assembly and speech in public spaces. *Guerilla Waves* challenges these restrictions through an illegal act that trespasses across the government's "nawabari."

Break it Before it's Broken　2015

In *They Do Not Understand Each Other* (2014), Kato recruits a South Korean man he met on the island of Tsushima to help him install a signboard on a nearby uninhabited island. Located between the Japanese archipelago and the Korean Peninsula, Tsushima has long been a flashpoint in international territorial disputes, which, of course, are the most fundamental version of "nawabari" struggles between nation-states. Unlike the perpetually circular and fruitless diplomatic negotiations between their respective countries, Kato and his South Korean counterpart's success in achieving a common goal despite mutual linguistic incomprehension mixes humor, irony, and a glimmer of hope for progress.

言葉が通じない／*They Do Not Understand Each Other* 2014

The COVID-19 pandemic opened a new angle in Kato's ongoing exploration of territory and boundaries. In February 2020, Kato traveled to Hong Kong to participate in *They Do Not Understand Each Other*, an exhibition at Tai Kwun Contemporary. Though the exhibition was postponed due to the pandemic and Kato was unable to return to Japan as planned, he was able to carry out *Superstring Secrets: Hong Kong* (2020), in which people were asked to write down and submit their "secrets" into a locked box. As tensions between the pro-democracy movement and the authorities escalated, Kato explored the ways in which the "psychological distance" created between people by secrets resonated with the "social distance" instituted during the pandemic to control the spread of infections. After Kato returned to Japan, he organized *Superstring Secrets: Tokyo* (2020), collecting secrets around the new sports facilities created for the Tokyo Olympics and Paralympics. That a sporting event intended to unify Japanese citizens and mark the nation's recovery from the 2011 disasters should have caused such a violent bifurcation in public opinion is tragically ironic.

Superstring Secrets: Hong Kong 2020

Superstring Secrets: Tokyo 2020

It is thus that Kato has cut to the heart of questions of territoriality within local society and politics, but in a form that everyone, regardless of where they are from or where they live, can understand and empathize with. To truly appreciate the diversity of the world, nothing is more important than mutual understanding and respect. Kato's work provides us with the hope and courage to believe that, despite the complex geopolitics of this planet, someday this world will be one in which everyone will be able to live permanently in peace. Tsubasa Kato's uniqueness as an artist lies in the ability of his critical insight to open up vistas through which we, as humans, might soar through the air unencumbered by turf and boundaries.

て、無人島にサインボードを立てる。対馬は日本列島と朝鮮半島の中間に位置し、その領有権をめぐる主張にはくい違いがみられる。領土をめぐる国際紛争は国家間の縄張り争いの最たるものだ。似たり寄ったりの主張を双方が応酬し合う不毛な外交交渉とは裏腹に、加藤と韓国人男性の2人が言葉の障壁を乗り越えてなんとか目的を達成する映像には、ユーモアと皮肉、そして一縷（いちる）の希望が入り混じる。

　新型コロナウイルスのパンデミックは、縄張りをめぐる加藤の思索に新たな視点を提供することになった。2020年2月、大館當代美術館（タイクン）の「言葉が通じない」展に参加するため、加藤は香港に滞在していた。展覧会は延期となり、帰国もままならない状況下で始めたのが、人々に「秘密」を投函してもらうプロジェクトだった。《**Superstring Secrets: Hong Kong**》(2020) は、民主化運動とそれに対する当局の取り締まりがエスカレートするなか、感染防止のための「社会的な距離（ソーシャルディスタンス）」ならぬ、人々の秘密によってできた「心理的な距離」に焦点を当てている。また、帰国後に制作した《**Superstring Secrets: Tokyo**》(2020) では、東京オリンピック・パラリンピックのため新設された競技施設の周辺で「秘密」が集められた。震災からの復興をアピールし、国民の一体感を醸成するはずだったスポーツの祭典が、開催の是非をめぐって世論を二分したことは皮肉としかいいようがない。

　このように加藤翼は、縄張りにまつわるローカルな社会や政治の問題に鋭く切り込み、それを世界中の誰もが共有しうる体験としてしなやかに提示する。私たちが生きる世界の多様性を真に理解するためには、相互理解と相互尊重が何よりも重要だろう。加藤の作品は、複雑に絡み合う地政学に覆われた大地を、誰もが安住できる持続可能な世界に変えるための勇気と希望を与えてくれる。縄張りや境界線のない大空を自由に飛翔するすぐれた洞察力と批評性こそ、加藤翼というアーティストのたぐい稀な作家性に違いない。

対談01　内部と外部のつながり

ケン・タダシ・オオシマ　×　加藤翼

翼：2015〜2017年のあいだ、僕はシアトルにあるワシントン大学建築学科のリサーチャーとして、日米で現代アートの風土にどの程度ギャップがあるかを比較・調査するためにアメリカに滞在していました。右も左も分からないまま生活を始めたわけですが、教授のケン・タダシ・オオシマさんにシアトルのアートピープルとつないでもらったり、イベントを紹介してもらったりすることで、徐々に制作を軌道に乗せていきました。そんな僕のシアトルでの日々を少なからず知るケンさんに、その専門である建築学の視点から僕のプロジェクトと今回の展覧会のインスタレーションについて光を当ててもらえるよう、お話したいと思います。

ケン：はい、今日はこうしてお話しできてうれしく思います。パフォーマンスとインスタレーションが交錯する翼さんの作品は、世界中のさまざまな環境や文化の影響を受けてきたと思います。時とともに作風が開花されていくにつれ、私はその点をとりわけ興味深く感じるようになりました。2011年3月11日に発生した東日本大震災から近年の新型コロナウイルスによるパンデミックに至るまでの期間は少し特別で、個人と集団が行動によって対話を図ろうとするとき、その時と場所に応じて独自のダイナミクスが生み出されてきました。特に翼さんが日米芸術家交換プログラムでシアトルのワシントン大学にいた2015年から2017年にかけては、そうしたダイナミクスを数多く目の当たりにしたことでしょう。その間アメリカはまさに重大な過渡期にあって、オバマ政権からトランプ政権へのシフトが起きました。私が翼さんの作品に惹きつけられる点はたくさんあるんですが、まずはアメリカにいた頃の経験が翼さんの考え方をどう形作ってきたのかについてお話ししてみましょうか。

内部者と外部者の関係性

翼：まずアメリカでのプロジェクトについて話す前に、僕がアメリカ行きを決意したところから始めると、2011年11月、まだ震災の傷跡が生々しい福島県いわき市の豊間地区というところで《**The Lighthouses-11.3 PROJECT**》というプロジェクトを実践したことがそれに直接的に影響しています。

　僕は震災の直後から豊間地区で瓦礫の撤去だとか食料の配布だとかの被災地支援活動をしていたんですけど、それを通じて徐々に地区のコミュニティとつながりが生まれていって、このプロジェクトに行き着きました。地区を含むその周辺地域で津波によって倒壊した家の跡から、瓦礫となった木材を集め、地域のシンボルである塩屋埼灯台（しおやざきとうだい）（津波で土台がダメージ

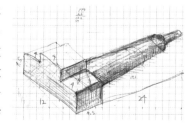

Tsubasa: Between 2015 and 2017, I was a researcher in the Department of Architecture at the University of Washington. I was in the United States to better understand how big the gap was between contemporary art there and in Japan. I didn't know anything about anything when I arrived, but thankfully Professor Ken Tadashi Oshima introduced me to people and events around Seattle's art scene, which helped me gradually get my art practice on track. So, Ken, given your familiarity with my time in Seattle, I was hoping today that you might shed some light on my work and the installation at Tokyo Opera City Art Gallery from the vantage of your field of expertise, architectural studies.

Ken: Well, it's my pleasure to join you today in conversation. Your work on the interplay between performance and installation has been informed by diverse contexts and cultures around the world, which I have found to be profoundly interesting as your practice has unfolded over time. In creating a dialogue between individual and communal action, unique dynamics emerge based on time/space that span the 3.11 disaster in Tohoku to the COVID-19 pandemic. In particular, you directly witnessed many of these dynamics while a fellow in the Japan-U.S. Exchange Friendship Program in the Arts, based in Seattle at the University of Washington from 2015 to 2017. That was certainly a momentous time in the United States, marking the shift between the Obama and Trump presidential administrations. There are many aspects of your work that fascinate me—perhaps we can begin with your time in the United States and how it shaped your thinking.

Between Insiders and Outsiders
Tsubasa: Before I talk about the projects I did in the United States, I want to say a few things about my decision to go there. In November 2011, I did a project titled *The Lighthouses – 11.3 PROJECT*. It happened in the Toyoma district of Iwaki, in southeastern Fukushima, at a time when the scars from the earthquake and tsunami were still fresh. My going to America was influenced by this project.
    Immediately after the disaster, as part of the recovery efforts, I helped with clearing debris and distributing food in Toyoma. The connections and friendships I made then served as the basis for the lighthouse project. I went around Toyoma and nearby areas to salvage junk lumber from houses destroyed by the tsunami and, with those materials, built an approximately 13.4-meter-high structure resembling the Shioyazaki Lighthouse, a local icon, the foundation of which had been damaged by the tsunami. The performance involved having locals from the area and

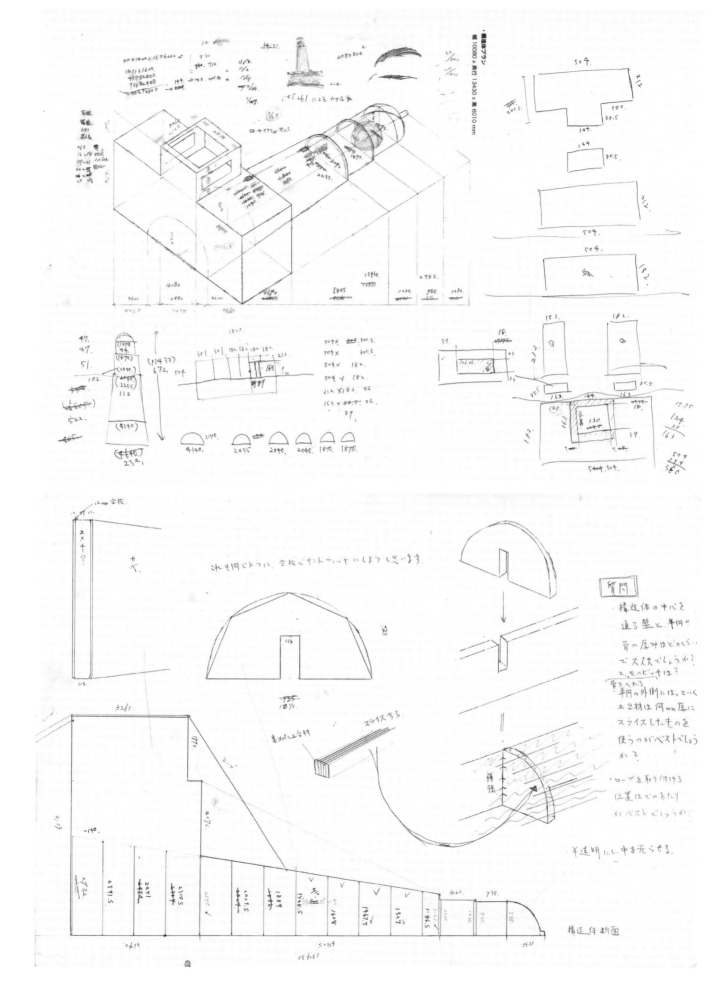

を受けて灯りが消えてしまっていました）をモチーフに13.4mくらいの構造体を制作して、当時、仮設住宅に避難している被災者の方々や地区の人たちと一緒にそれをロープで引き起こすパフォーマンスをやったんです。3月11日を反転させた11月3日の文化の日に。このプロジェクトのために半年間ほど地区で活動していると、そこでいろんな境遇の被災者と出会うわけですね。家も家族も仕事もなくしてしまった人もいれば、原発事故の影響で双葉町や大熊町から避難してきた人もたくさんいた。プロジェクトは瓦礫材を使うので、当初は震災の中でも津波という天災に対峙するコンセプトだったのですが、福島県内の帰還困難区域から避難してきた人々と会うにつれて少しずつ原発事故についても考え始めたわけです。

　東京電力の原子力発電所が福島で爆発したことで、住民がその土地から追われる。悲惨な結果を生んだ原発事故は、その土地に住んでいない外部者が、そこにもともと住んでいた内部者に与えた悪影響の最たるものだと思います。外の人間によって自分の家から追い出されるという決定的な出来事に対して、被害者は為す術もありません。そして原発問題が難しいのは、たとえ被害者の人たちだけでなく、僕たち外の（東京の）人間の多くが原発を拒否したとしても、その未来を容易に裁量できないほどに大きな問題であり、そんなふうに問題のサイズが大きくなればなるほど僕たちに（回答権はあっても）決定権はないかもしれないということです。

　原発は国家の核心的な政治プロジェクトであり、海外企業とも密接につながっている国際的プロジェクトでもある。実際に福島第一原発の原子炉はアメリカのGEが設計・開発したものだったりして、すでに日本人という「内部者」だけで完結できる問題でもない。福島の事例から端的に明らかになったこうした矛盾、というか、入れ子構造になる内部者と外部者の関係性というのは、現代のグローバリゼーションが突き進んでいった結果の表れだと僕は感じました。それを見極めるためにというか、グローバリゼーションが地域社会や国家といった共同体（コミュニティ）のフレームをどのように刺激したり揺り動かしたりしているのかをちゃんと考えるために、その本尊とも言えるアメリカに行こうと思ったんです。

refugees living in the temporary emergency housing blocks pull and raise the structure with ropes. It took place on Culture Day, November 3 (11.3), which is to say, the inverse of March 11 (3.11). In preparation, I spent about six months doing different things and meeting all sorts of people whose lives had been impacted by the disaster. Some people had lost not just their homes, but also family members and their jobs. Others, many others, were refugees from places like Futaba and Okuma that had been evacuated after the meltdowns at the Fukushima Daiichi Nuclear Power Plant. As the lighthouse project used junk lumber, it was most immediately about the tsunami as a natural disaster. But since I also had a lot of contact with people evacuated from the exclusion zones in Fukushima, I started thinking about the nuclear disaster as well.

After the explosions at the Fukushima Daiichi plant, residents from surrounding areas were ordered to leave their homes and land. Since the plant is run by Tokyo Electric Power Company (TEPCO), one could say that people from the area were made to suffer the worst possible outcome of something brought to the area by outsiders. There wasn't anything local people could do about losing their homes at the hands of outsiders. What's tricky about the issue of nuclear power is that, even if a lot of outsiders like myself (people from Tokyo) oppose nuclear power, the scale of the problem is so great that no one really knows what's going to happen in the future. The bigger a problem gets, the less right any one party has to make decisions about it, regardless of whether or not they have the right to *say* something about it.

Nuclear power is fundamentally a project of the nation-state. At the same time, it is international in character because of necessary links with foreign industries. The reactors at Fukushima Daiichi, for example, were designed and built by GE, an American company. In other words, nuclear power plants were never something that could be managed by "insiders,"

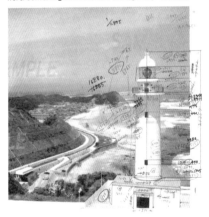

by Japanese, alone. Fukushima is a clear and extreme example of this contradiction, and it made me start thinking about how intensified globalization produces nested relationships between outsiders and insiders. I went to the United States also to better understand the way globalization influences and shapes local and state-level communities. America, after all, has been the prime driver of this paradigm.

ケン：かつて、原子力発電に移行しようという動きはまさに世界的に広がっていました。ここワシントン州でも、1968年に計画の立ち上がったサトソップ原子力発電所の建設が1977年に始まりました。ところが、1979年に起きたペンシルベニア州のスリーマイル島原子力発電所の部分的なメルトダウン事故に加え、地元の財政的・政治的問題により、この発電所の建設は何十年も遅れたまま放置されています。もしもサトソップが完成していたなら、ワシントン州も福島と同じように津波が襲った際に大災害となるリスクがあったでしょう。2007年に合意されたアメリカのGEと日本の日立製作所との原子力事業における提携も表すように、私たちはたしかにグローバリゼーションが進んだ世の中にいますが、直接体験しなければ本当の意味では理解できないその土地固有のストーリーが数多くあります。

翼：アメリカに向かうときはまさか大統領選（2016年）を間近で目撃することになるとは思ってなかったんですが、トランプ大統領の誕生はまさしくグローバリゼーションがもたらしたダイナミクスの産物でもあると同時に、アメリカ社会の行き過ぎたポリティカル・コレクトネスへの反動だとも言われていました。そのとき僕はシアトルのノース・ビーコン・ヒルのシェアハウスで10人のアメリカ人たちと暮らしていて、そのほとんどがローカルの若い白人ミュージシャンたちでした。2016年11月8日の投票日には一緒にテレビの前でその結果に唖然としながらも、その中の1人が、アメリカで白人として生活することのジレンマみたいなものは確かにある、と率直に吐露したのがとても意外でした。たとえば、彼が浴衣を着てその写真をInstagramにアップしたら過度のポリコレ監視者から（文化盗用として）批判され炎上してしまうかもしれないので、常にそうした言動を取らないよう抑制しているらしいんです。そのような、周囲から常に白人として見られることへのプレッシャーはアジア人である僕にとっては想像したこともない視点でした。SNSの普及によって他者と簡単につながり合ってしまう反面、行き過ぎたポリコレ監視によってマジョリティであるほど拘束もし合っているんじゃないかと考えて、この現代のジレンマをテーマにシアトルで《**Woodstock 2017**》を制作しました。

Woodstock 2017 2017

これは4人のミュージシャンがお互いに縛られながら／縛りながらアメリカ国歌を演奏するという作品です。彼らがその同居人だったミュージシャンたちで、彼ら

Ken: The initial movement towards nuclear power was indeed global. Even here, in Washington state, we have the Satsop Nuclear Power Plant, the initial plans of which date to 1968, with construction beginning in 1977. However, the partial meltdown of the Three Mile Island Nuclear Plant in Pennsylvania in 1979, compounded by financial and political problems locally, delayed its progress for decades. Had Satsop been completed, Washington state would have been just as vulnerable to disaster from a tsunami as Fukushima was. Though we live in a globalized world—GE's alignment with Hitachi from 2007, for example—there are so many local stories that can only really be understood through direct experience.

Tsubasa: When I departed for the United States, I had no idea that I'd be witnessing the 2016 American presidential election from close-up. Trump's rise was a product of the dynamics of globalization, at the same time that it was a reaction to the perceived extremes of political correctness. In Seattle, I lived in a house together with ten Americans, in the neighborhood of North Beacon Hill. Most of them were local musicians, and young and white. Everyone was shocked as we watched the election results live on television together on November 8, 2016. I remember one of them talking about the contradictions of living as a white person in America. For example, about how they had to be careful about what they posted online, because if you posted, say, a photograph of yourself in a yukata on Instagram, you might get canceled for cultural appropriation by someone who is overly PC. As an Asian, it never occurred to me that white people might be watching and pressuring other white people like that. The spread of social media has made it easier for us to connect with others, but it has also created a situation in which the majority culture is restricting itself in different ways through extreme forms of PC policing. That's what *Woodstock 2017* (2017) was about, which I made while I was in Seattle.

In this work, there are four musicians trying to play the *Star-Spangled Banner* while being tied with ropes to one another. While they're restraining others, they're also restrained *by* others. All four of them were my roommates. I shot the performance in an industrial area where their studio was located. The title, of course, refers to the legendary Woodstock music festival of 1969, at the end of which Jimi Hendrix, who was from Seattle, played a guitar solo of the national anthem in front of 400,000 hippies and young Americans. In contrast to the passion of that event, I wanted to show that, in the present, the more we are actually connected to one another, the harder it is to achieve anything in common. Therefore, the national anthem, ostensibly a symbol of unity, should be played in a context of mutual restraint and tension. That was the inspiration behind the performance.

Ken: I think collective power, whether it be of your "pull and raise/topple" series or the musicians in *Woodstock 2017*, is an important aspect of what your work represents. I find your explanation very interesting in terms of how we connect on different levels, and not just physically,

のスタジオのあるシアトルの工業地帯で撮影しました。作品タイトルはもちろん、1969年に開かれた伝説的な野外音楽フェス、ウッドストック・フェスティバルをもとにしています。新しい時代を求めるヒッピーや若者たち40万人が結集したこのフェスの最後に、シアトル出身のジミ・ヘンドリックスが登場してアメリカ国歌をギターソロで演奏したんですが、その熱狂とは対比的に、直接つながってしまえばしまうほどひとつのゴールを共有するのが難しくなっている現代においては、統合の象徴である国歌というものはお互いに縛り合う緊張関係の中で演奏されるべきではないか。そんな考えから、この作品を作ったんです。

ケン：「引き倒し・引き興し」シリーズであれ《**Woodstock 2017**》であれ、集団の発揮する力はあなたの作品の中できわめて重要な要素だと私は思っています。いま説明を聞いていてあらためて興味深いと思ったのは、私たちはさまざまな次元においてすでにつながっているということです。3.11の震災時に津波が、同じ環太平洋地域に連なるここワシントン州にまで到達したような意味においてだけでなく、私たちは過去のさまざまな出来事を通じて、物理的にも心理的にも、グローバルにつながっているのです。移民から成るアメリカという国での人々のつながり方は世界でも特に珍しいものだと思いますが、その多様性こそまさにトランプ政権期に大きな試練を迎えたものでした。

Abandon (Grand Canyon) 2013

　日本だと大きな集団やグループの一員であったり、協働して何かをしたりという意識がより強いと思うんですが、それとは対照的に、ここアメリカでは、個人や個性にもっと多くの重心が置かれます。それが、シアトルでの《**Woodstock 2017**》やノースダコタでの《**Black Snake**》といったあなたの作品を見ると、この両文化のあいだにある壁は見事に打ち砕かれていて、集団的な経験の新たなあり様がアメリカでもその顔を覗かせている。こうした「つながり」、あるいは、文化をまたいで私たちがどのようにつながったりつながれなかったりするのかについて、翼さんの考えを知りたいです。

翼：《**Black Snake**》という作品にいたる話をしましょう。シアトルに滞在する前

such as with the 3.11 disaster and the Pacific Rim, and the tsunami waves reaching all the way to Washington state. We are also connected in a global way or through historical events, mentally as well as physically. The way we connect to one another in the US, as a land of immigrants, could be considered particularly unique–though that has been explicitly challenged during the period of the Trump administration.

In Japan, there is greater consciousness of being part of a collective group or actively cooperating to make something happen. By contrast, in America, much more importance is placed on individuals and individuality. I find that your work powerfully breaks the barrier between these two cultures, so, for example, you broach collective experience in **Woodstock 2017** in Seattle or **Black Snake** in North Dakota. I'm curious about your thoughts on this "connectedness," and how we connect and not connect among cultures.

Tsubasa: Let's talk about **Black Snake**, then. In 2013, before I lived in Seattle, I took a road trip around the United States, departing from New York. Seeing a lot of abandoned materials along the side of the road–cars, boats, houses–I decided to try to pull them down or over with ropes. This became the photo series **Abandon**. It was part of my research into how globalization expressed itself inside the United States.

It was on that trip that I first went to the Standing Rock Reservation in North Dakota and met people of the Sioux tribe. When I set out, talking to indigenous peoples was not on my itinerary, but in doing so I learned about how Native Americans had been pushed off their land and put into reservations across the country, places where the history of tensions between native insiders and immigrant outsiders is very stark. Similar histories of invasion and resistance can be found in Japan between the Yamato peoples and the indigenous Ainu and Ryukyuans, as they can between different countries in Asia. But in talking with members of the Sioux, I felt that their attachment to the land and notions of community were very similar to how Japanese think about "nativeness." To put it abstractly, there's a similar vibe with regards to how people think about locality, family, and one's proximity to nature, and about festivals and animistic beliefs, as products of historical and cultural accretion. Anyway, I decided I

Abandon (South Dakota) 2013

Abandon (Monument Valley) 2013

の2013年、僕はニューヨークを起点にアメリカを一周しました。その道端で見つけたアバンダンド・マテリアル、つまり捨てられて放置された車や家や船、そういった物体にロープをかけて引っ張る姿を収めた写真シリーズ《Abandon》を撮り溜めていったのは、アメリカにおいてグローバリゼーションがどういう形で現れているのかをリサーチする作業の一環でもありました。

その道すがら、ノースダコタ州のスタンディングロック居留地に立ち止まってネイティブアメリカンのスー族の人たちに出会うわけです。まさか途中で彼女／彼ら先住民と話をするなんて思ってもみなかったんですが、聞けばネイティブアメリカンが押しやられている居留地はアメリカ全土に散らばっていて、それはもともとの土地に住んでいた内部者と、そこにあとからやって来た外部者との軋轢の歴史でもある。もちろんそういう侵略と抵抗の歴史は日本でもアイヌや琉球の人々と倭人とのあいだ、あるいはアジア諸国とのあいだにあるわけですが、彼女／彼たちと話していくと、自らの土地やコミュニティに対する意識が日本の土着性とすごく通じていると感じたんです。抽象的ですが、地元や家族の捉え方だとか自然との距離感だとか、お祭りやアニミズム的な信仰といった、歴史や文化の一つひとつの積み重ねから生まれる雰囲気。《Abandon》シリーズを終えたらまたここに戻ってきてプロジェクトを起こそうと決めました。

それで最初に実現したのが2013年の《Boarding School》です。これも「引き倒し・引き興し」に連なる作品ですが、構築物のモチーフはタイトル通り「寄宿学校」です。開拓者たちによって自由な移動を制限され、居留地に移住させられたネイティブアメリカンの子供たちは、これも強制的に親元から離されて「寄宿学校」に住まわされ、そこで自らの言語・習慣を否定する同化的な英語教育を徹底的に施されました。こうした同化政策はカナダでも行なわれ、先日、カナダのサスカチワン州にあった寄宿学校跡地から750以上もの墓標のない墓が発見されるというショッキングなニュースがあったばかりです。スタンディングロックの中心地、

Boarding School 2013

フォート・イエーツにあるスー族の本部オフィスの目と鼻の先の空き地でそのBoarding Schoolを地元スー族の人たちと一緒にロープで引っ張って倒したんです。1か月半くらい、居留地内の家々に泊まらせてもらって彼らの生活や慣習、歴史に

would have to return to Standing Rock after finishing the *Abandon* project.

The first related project I completed was *Boarding School*, in 2013, which is part of my "pull and raise/ topple" series. As the title suggests, the structure manipulated in the performance is a model of a boarding school, like the many set up by white settlers to separate Native American children from their parents. While the parents weren't allowed free movement and were confined to reservations, at the schools the children were banned from speaking their native language and practicing native customs, and were subjected to an English-language education program designed to assimilate them into settler culture. Similar assimilation policies were undertaken in Canada. In fact, just recently, they discovered more than 750 unmarked graves on the site of a former boarding school in Saskatchewan. It was shocking news. In Fort Yates, the main settlement in Standing Rock, we installed my model of the boarding school in an empty lot directly across from where the Sioux tribe's administrative headquarters is, and, together with local Sioux, pulled down the structure using ropes. I spent about a month and a half inside the reservation, staying in people's homes, learning about their lives, their customs, and their history, and eventually negotiating who would be involved in the project, where I could work on it, where the performance would be held, et cetera.

Boarding School 2013

This was the first full-scale project I executed in the United States, and while I was working on it I came to realize something important in common across my "pull and raise/topple" projects, including those I had done in Japan. Without doing fieldwork or making connections with locals, it's impossible to come up with an appropriate architectural structure or carry out the performance successfully. But even before that, you have to think about physical issues, about weight. For example, if a structure is too big and heavy and requires more people to lift it, that itself can inspire people who might have just been spectators to join in and become participants. And if there are still not

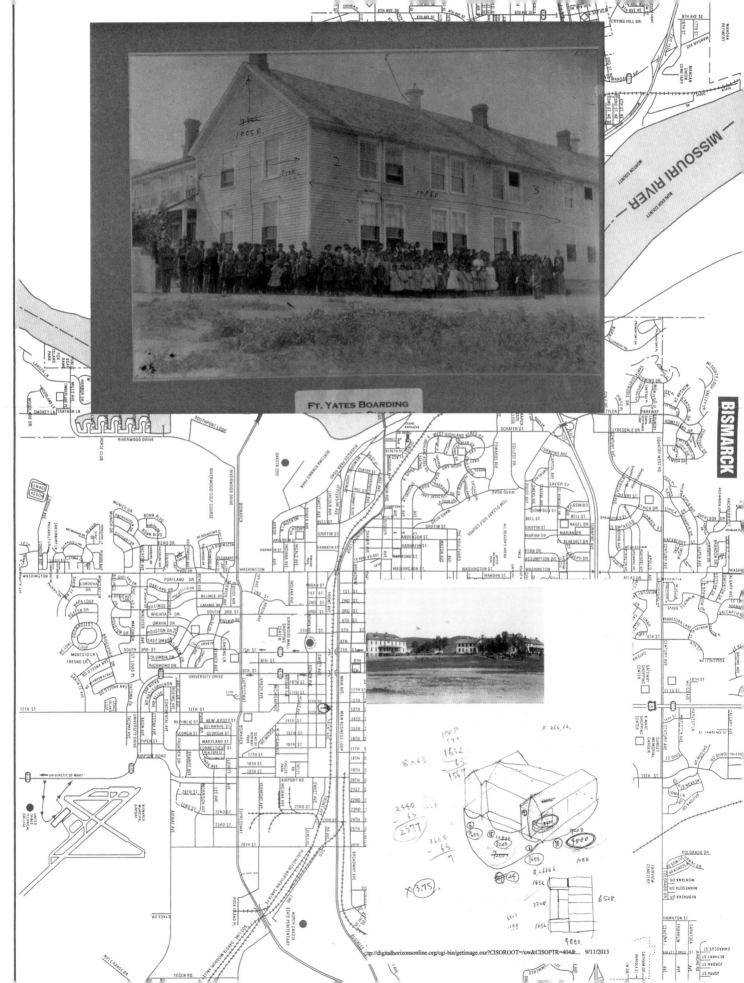

FT. YATES BOARDING

ついて聞きながら、制作する場所や人手、パフォーマンス場所など、一つひとつ交渉しながら進めていきました。

　これがアメリカでの初プロジェクトだったのですが、実際やってみると日本でも重ねてきた「引き倒し・引き興し」が共通に持っているひとつの特質が浮かび上がってきました。構築物のモチーフはその土地のフィールドワークから発想し、地元の人たちとつながりを作らないと実際のパフォーマンスまで行き着かないのですが、結局はフィジカリティ、重さという現実に引き戻されていくことがわかったんです。たとえば構築物が重すぎて引き起こすにはもっと人が必要だとなったときにはじめて、今まで鑑賞者だった人たちも参加者に切り替わって、それでも人が足りなければ周りの人たちが人を呼びにいって、その合算された力が構築物の重さを超えたときに、ようやくその物体が起き上がって、倒れる。

　自分たちを支配していた「Boarding School」を引き起こして倒す、ってとても象徴的でメッセージ性のある行為ですよね。でも、それに携わった参加者／当事者たちがどこまでそれを自覚しているのかはほとんどわからない。「これはいったい何なの？」「私たち、いま何をやってるの？」という質問が来ればすぐ背景のストーリーを説明するんですが、その共同行為に飛び込むための直接的なきっかけは説明的なコンテクストというよりは、いま目の前で起こっていることに対する身体的なリアクションなんですよね。

ケン：フィジカルは言葉を超越すると思います。つまり、その「引き起こす／引き倒す」という身体的動作が言葉よりも多くのことを伝えている。政治なんかと違って物理的な強さや重さが最も重要視されるとき、ある種の人間性が作用するはずです。「引き倒し・引き興し」シリーズをはじめとする翼さんの作品が、異なる文化や地域をパワフルに超越していける理由はそこだと思います。

　とはいえ、スタンディングロックはあまりにも遠く――同じアメリカの東海岸や西海岸からも遠いのですが――日本とはあまりにもかけ離れています。その広大な見晴らしは月面風景のようでさえある。そこでの体験は（先ほどの発言のように）自分にとって近いところと異質な部分が同居するものだったと思います。翼さんはその体験を実際どのように感じましたか？　まるで疎遠な場所にいるように感じたのか、それとも、人々とのつながりを持てる馴染み深さを感じたのか。

翼：少しずつコミュニティとの関係性を築いてその距離を縮めていった、というのが実際のところですね。まず地元の人を一人紹介してもらって話を聞いて、その人に別の人を紹介してもらってまた話を聞いて、また紹介してもらうっていう、その繰り返し。コミュニティの外から来た僕一人 vs 地域住民という構造じゃなくて、できるかぎり一対一で対話をしながらネットワークを作っていく。もちろん最初は、ずいぶん遠いところまで来たなという感覚です。スタンディングロックを初めて訪れたときは冬でマイナス 20 度でしたし（笑）。でもだんだん話をしていくなかでコミュニティの一員になっていくような感覚ができてきて、最終的には近い関係性に行き着くわけです。

　その後スタンディングロックは 2016 年の大統領選のときに「#NoDAPL」で世間から注目されます。ダコタ・アクセス・パイプライン（Dakota Access Pipeline）と

enough people, then they'll call for help from others in the area. Once you've amassed enough human strength to overcome the weight, that's when the structure raises up and then falls.

The performance in **Boarding School** is obviously symbolic, by having the very people who were oppressed by boarding schools working together to raise and topple the structure. Of course, it's hard to say to what extent the participants were actually conscious of that symbolism. If they asked, "What is this thing? What exactly are we doing here?," we'd always take the time to explain the background of the project. But the immediate context of why they threw themselves into the collective action of the performance was not the background history or the symbolism, it's the physical response of wanting to take part in something that's happening in front of you.

Ken: I think the physical transcends language. That is, through the actual pulling activity, you can communicate even more than through words. There's a certain humanity involved when strength and weight become primary, more than with other aspects, like politics. I think that's what makes your work, such as the "pull and raise" and "pull and topple" series, so powerful in its ability to transcend different cultures and places.

Yet, Standing Rock is so far away—even from the east and west coasts of the US, it's far away—and so different from Japan. The landscape there is vast and wide open, almost like a moonscape. The experience must have been both familiar and foreign to you. I wonder how you actually experienced that? Did it feel like you were in a remote place, or were things familiar enough that you could connect with people?

Tsubasa: By gradually building personal relations with the community, I do feel that I was able to shorten that distance to some extent. You meet one person, get to know them, they introduce you to someone else, you get to know them, they introduce you to someone else, and so on. I didn't go in as an outsider trying to appeal to the local community as a whole. I slowly built up a network one-on-one with different people. Of course, initially I felt like I couldn't have been further away from home than I was. After all, the first time I went to Standing Rock it was in the winter and like 20°C below zero! But after I was there for a while and talked to different people, I started feeling like I was part of the community in a way. I felt pretty close to everyone by the time I left.

After that, during the 2016 presidential race, Standing Rock received a lot of attention because of #NoDAPL, the movement against the construction of the underground Dakota Access Pipeline, part of which was slated to run through Standing Rock. With locals mounting largescale protests and clashing with state police, it became a key issue during the election. The person who started #NoDAPL on social media was the daughter of someone who participated in **Boarding School**, and a lot of the people I met during that project got involved in the protest movement. When Trump won, he immediately gave the green light for construction on the pipeline. Right in the middle of that was when I went back to Standing Rock and did **Black**

Black Snake 2017

いう地下石油パイプラインを作る計画がもともとあって、その一部がスタンディングロックを通過するので住民たちが大きな抗議デモを起こして州兵と衝突し、選挙のひとつの争点というかキープレイスになったんです。「#NoDAPL」のキャンペーンをSNSで始めたのは2013年の《**Boarding School**》に協力してくれた人の娘で、他にもプロジェクトで知り合った人たちがたくさんデモに参加していた。結果的にトランプが勝って就任直後に建設工事が始まるんですが、その渦中に現地を再訪して行なったのが《**Black Snake**》です。彼女／彼らが皮肉を込めて「黒い蛇」と呼ぶパイプラインを黒いプラスチックシートで見立ててグリッド状の構築物に張り巡らせて、それをみんなで引き倒しました。

　抗議デモのキャンプ地になっていたのはスタンディングロックの東端、ミズーリ川の近くで、そこに建設会社のブルドーザーに対抗するように全米から何千というサポーターが駆けつけ、メディアも大挙していました。でもその影響で川のほとりに棲んでいたプレーリードッグ（注＊体長30〜40cmほど、ネズミのような見た目のリス科の動物。北米の草原地帯に穴を掘って巣穴を作り、群れで生活する）は住処を奪われて、丘を超えてこちら側の草原──広大なスタンディングロックの平原の一角に、2013年のプロジェクトの際に作業所として使わせてもらったネイティブアメリカンの友人の裏庭というか裏山がありました──に避難してきたという話をその友人から聞いて、すごく象徴的な現われだなと思ったんです。それが《**Underground Orchestra**》というプロジェクトのきっかけです。

Underground Orchestra 2017

　このプレーリードッグたちもネイティブアメリカンたちと同じく、外部から来た人間たちによって住処を奪われて、人知れずここに大移動してきたわけです。おかげで、かつての牧歌的な草原の風景は無数の穴ぼことトンネルに様変わりしていましたが、僕にはそれが彼女／彼らによる人間全体へのデモのように見えたんです。地上を眺めているだけでは捉えられないこのプレーリードッグたちの地下活動を、音に変換して記録することにしました。巣穴に100個ほど鈴を打ち付けておくと、彼女らが出たり入ったりするときに鈴が鳴る。それを録音機で何度も繰り返し録音して彼女らの鳴き声とともに文字通り「地下のオーケストラ」として「演奏」化した映像作品です。これは今回の展示インスタレーションの核になる作品のひとつで、

Snake. Everyone there referred to the pipeline jokingly as the "black snake." So, we built this gridded structure, wove a large black plastic sheet through it like a snake, then got everyone together to pull and topple it over.

The protest camp was located on the east side of Standing Rock, near the Missouri River. Thousands of people from across the US went there to oppose the bulldozers that were there for the construction of the pipeline. The media was also in force. That same area, near the river, used to be inhabited by prairie dogs, but they were chased from their homes by everything that was going on. Then a friend of mine told me—someone I met in 2013 and who let me use what was essentially his backyard, a tiny corner of the vast plain that makes up Standing Rock, to do work on *Boarding School*—he told me that the prairie dogs had taken up residence on the back side of the hill behind his house. I thought that was really symbolic. That led to *Underground Orchestra*.

Like Native Americans, you might say, the prairie dogs had been chased from their homes by outsiders, a mass migration occurring below the radar of human consciousness. The once-pastoral landscape of the plain was thus turned into a network of tunnels, which I came to think about as a mass protest against humanity itself. Since it wasn't visible from the surface, I had the idea of translating and recording the prairie dogs' underground movement into sound. We installed over a hundred small bells at the entrances to their tunnels, which rang every time they went in or out. We spent hours and hours trying to record the sound of the bells ringing, combined that with the chirping noise the prairie dogs make, resulting in a literal "underground orchestra," essentially a video-based musical performance. Since, like *The Lighthouses – 11.3 PROJECT*, I think *Underground Orchestra* really captures the relationship between insiders and outsiders, I made it one of the focal works in the installation at Tokyo Opera City Art Gallery.

Physical/Virtual Connections
Ken: *Underground Orchestra* is also interesting in terms of "underground" culture. In English, that might mean underground music or varieties of alternative culture. But here, in your work, it is literally "under the ground." There's something very metaphorical as well as physical about the world of these prairie dogs. There's a game called "whack-a-mole" in which you have to hit plastic moles with a club, but it's impossible to win because they keep popping up faster and faster. And in some ways, that's like life itself. I think it represents so much of our existence not only in natural or political environments, but also in many complex social situations.

It would be interesting for you to come back to the US now in 2021, for this next chapter in history after Trump, since policies regarding the pipeline and the environment are changing once again. And also after this year-and-a-half with COVID-19, where we were distanced and find it difficult to connect with each other. Your work makes viewers think about human connections, and though we talk a lot about virtual connections through social media or through electronic

福島の《**The Lighthouses - 11.3 PROJECT**》から続く、外部者と内部者との関係性をよく映し出していると思っています。

フィジカル／バーチャルなコネクション

ケン：《**Underground Orchestra**》という作品は「アンダーグラウンドな」カルチャーという意味でも面白いと思いました。英語だとその語は、アンダーグラウンド・ミュージックだとかオルタナティブなカルチャーのことを指したりもしますが、あなたの作品の中では文字通り「地下」という意味になっている。そして、フィジカルなプレーリードッグの世界を描きながらも比喩的な意味合いがそこには含まれていますよね。連想したのは「もぐらたたき」というゲームで、出てきては消える「もぐら」をいくら叩いても「勝つ」ことのないそれは、ある意味人生そのもののようです。この作品は自然や政治の中にいる、そして複雑な社会のいろんな局面に生きる私たちの存在を表しているように思うのです。

　トランプ時代が終わり、パイプラインや環境問題にまつわる政策が再び変更されている2021年のいま、次の章へと進んでいるアメリカに翼さんがまた戻ってきたら面白いと思います。1年半にわたるコロナとの日々によって人々が互いに距離を取り、つながりを持ちにくくなった世界に。あなたの作品を見ると人間同士のつながりについて考えさせられるし、昨今はソーシャルメディアやデジタルを介した、いわゆるバーチャルなつながりがよく話題にのぼるけれど、パンデミックの収束に向けてリアルで物理的・身体的なつながりがますます大切になってくると思うんです。アメリカだけじゃなくて香港で過ごした時間も振り返ってみて、翼さんはこの「ディスタンス」の時期に「つながり」についての考えが変わったりしましたか？

香港の地下通路

翼：香港ではスタンディングロックとは別のかたちでデモが2019年から加熱していたんですが、コロナのパンデミックの影響でそれが少し静かになった2020年2月当時、香港に滞在していた僕はプロジェクトを進めていました。プレーリードッグじゃないんですけど（笑）、香港の街のアンダーグラウンドにもトンネル（地下道）

media in general, it seems like physical or real connections will become more important again as we recover from the pandemic. Looking back not only to America but also to your time in Hong Kong, how has this period of distancing changed your thinking about "connections"?

Tsubasa: In Hong Kong, the pro-democracy protests have been really intense since 2019, though, of course, they're very different from those in Standing Rock. When I went to Hong Kong in February 2020, the protests had cooled a bit because of the pandemic. Hong Kong has this network of underground tunnels—no prairie dogs, though!—with information about demonstrations, political manifestos, graffiti and political slogans, all written and pasted on the walls, which the authorities came along and got rid of periodically. But after they erase them or rip them down, they leave these traces on the walls. The interesting thing is that it's the same on the internet. The protests mainly grew by exchanging information on social media, which the authorities are constantly checking and censoring. I was interested in the structural similarity between the two.

So, for the project that became *Superstring Secrets: Hong Kong*, I first placed these white postbox-like receptacles at various places in the underground tunnels for people to put their "secrets" in. Since in the

Superstring Secrets: Hong Kong - Tai Wo 2020

Superstring Secrets: Hong Kong - Fo Tan 2020

が張り巡らされていて、時節柄そこにデモの情報やステートメントが、グラフィティ的なものから直接に政治的なメッセージまで、いろいろと書かれたり貼られたりしていくんですが、結局それらは全部消されるんです。書いては消されて、貼っては剝がされて、僕らはそういうトレース（痕跡）だけ目にするわけですが、興味深いことにそれはネット上でも同じなんです。基本的にSNSでの情報交換によって拡大する香港のデモでは、同時にそうしたメッセージが当局の検閲・チェックを受けて消されていく。その構造的な同質性に大きな関心を持ちました。

　のちに《Superstring Secrets：Hong Kong》として結実する作品のために僕はまず、白いポストボックスみたいなものを地下通路に複数設置して「秘密」を集めることから始めました。背景に何かが取り消された跡がある、つまり表現の自由に密接に関わる空間の中で、行き交う人々に自身の秘密を紙に書いて投函してもらう。でもそれはあくまで「情報」なので、僕の今までの制作アプローチと比べればフィジカリティがないというか、直接的な接触や重さがないですよね。誰が書いたかわからない秘密。でもその情報の蓄積をなんとか受肉化したいと思い、大量に集めた秘密の紙をシュレッダーにかけて、それを撚り合わせてひとつの大きなロープを編み上げるというパフォーマンスを行ないました。

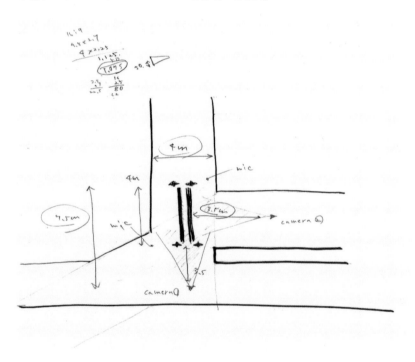

　この作業をよく見るとパフォーマー5人——彼女／彼らは現地のアーティストや学者、学生なのですが——がかぶっているヘルメットが棒でつながっていて、それで2mのソーシャルディスタンスが保たれています（笑）。ここに「connection（接続／つながり）」に関わる大きな変化があって、コロナ前の《Woodstock 2017》のパフォーマーのあいだにもロープでわたされた距離（ディスタンス）はあったものの、それは遠くなったり近くなったり伸縮可能なものだった。けれど《Superstring Secrets》ではその距離は完全に固定されたままです。つまり不自由は距離の増減ではなく距離の固定によって生じているように見える。なので「physical

background are the physical traces of messages that have been erased, the physical context is one intimately connected to issues of freedom of speech. In that space, we asked passersby to write down a secret on a piece of paper and put them in the boxes. The written secrets are just "information." Compared to how I had been making art previously, the physical wasn't that important to this project. There's no direct physical contact or weight involved. No one knows who wrote the secrets. But I wanted to give some kind of physical form to that accumulation of information, so I put all the written secrets we collected into a paper shredder and then twisted the shreds into a giant rope. That was the performance.

If you look carefully at the video, you'll see that the five performers—a philosopher, two artists, and two students in Hong Kong—are wearing helmets attached to one another with 2-meter pipes. That's to ensure they maintain proper social distance! This was a fundamentally different way of working with "connections" for me. For **Woodstock 2017**, which I made before the pandemic, there's distance between the performers, which is marked out by the rope connecting them, which gets tight or slack as they get further away or closer to one another. For **Superstring Secrets**, on the other hand, the distance between performers is fixed. Rather than increased distance resulting in decreased freedom, fixed distance results in lack of freedom. Put in terms of "physical connection," for my "pull and raise/topple" series, there's an actual physical structure at the center of the performances, which is pulled up and/or pulled over by a physical connection, meaning the ropes and the collective manipulation of them. When I went to the US, that central object was the national anthem. In Hong Kong, it was people's secrets. The performances are structured such that the performers around each "center" lose their freedom through relationships of distance.

Of course, there's still a physical dimension remaining in **Superstring Secrets**, probably because that's what I most believe in. Still, I'm interested in your question about doing projects in which connections are virtual rather than physical…

Wait, I have done one! **Can You Hear Me?** (2015) dates from before the pandemic, but what I did was line up four smartphone-sized LCD screens, each one showing a video of a single person. If you listen to the audio, you'll notice that the people are talking to one another by phone and then they start throwing stones. What's happening here is that the four people are in four different cities—Kota Kinabalu in Malaysia, Seattle, Mexico City, and Boston—and I had them all throw stones at the same time. It's just them throwing stones while on the phone, which looks simple. But from their perspective, since they can't see what the other people are doing, they can only guess when, or whether or not, anybody else is actually throwing their stones. Since this work is about synchronicity and collectivity through communication networks, I guess you could say it's related to questions about the virtual. Maybe if I increased the number of locations to forty or fifty, this experiment would have some potential.

connection（物理的つながり）」についていえば、一連の「引き倒し・引き興し」では物理的な構造体がパフォーマンスの中心にあって、それを物理的なつながり（ロープによる共同作業）によって引き倒し／引き起こしたわけですけど、アメリカではその中心は国歌になり、香港では人々の秘密に変化して、その中心を取り巻くパフォーマーたちは距離によってどんどん自由を奪われていくという構造になっています。

　でもこの《Superstring Secrets》にはまだフィジカリティが残っていますよね。もちろんそれは僕が最終的にフィジカリティを信じてしまっているからなんですけど、ケンさんの質問にあったようなバーチャルな接続／つながりに振りきったプロジェクトが可能かどうかは自分でも興味がありますね……。

　あっ、ひとつありました！　この《Can You Hear Me?》はコロナ禍の前の（2015年の）作品なんですけど、携帯電話サイズの液晶画面が４つ並べられていて、その中に１人ずつ立っています。音を聞くと、別々の場所から互いに電話で会話しているのがわかり、そしてみな同時に石を投げ始める。実際に、マレーシアのコタキナバル、シアトル、メキシコシティ、ボストンの４都市で同時刻に一斉に投石してもらいました。これは単純に電話しながら石を投げているだけなんですが、投げる本人の視点からすると（目の前にいない）相手がいま本当に石を投げているかどうかは想像するしかない。通信を土台にして同時性と共同性はあるんですが、たしかにこの作品は直接的にはつながっていないひとつの例かもしれないですね。単純なだけに、今後40か所とか50か所とかに場所を増やしていける、発展性のある作品だなと思っています。

Can You Hear Me? 2015

ケン：この作品をいまこうして見返すと、まるで現在の私たちのバーチャルなZoom 世界の先駆けのようで面白いですね。私の講義でもいまやこの景色は普通で、台湾、日本、ロサンゼルス、テキサスにいる学生たちがみんな画面越しに集まります。翼さんはもしかしてこんな現実を予見していたのかもしれないですね！　ここではバーチャルなつながりとリアルなつながりとのバランスがすごく大事になってきます。先ほど、パンデミックが収まったあとにはフィジカルなつながりがさらに重要になるだろうと言いましたが、私たちはこの世界をひとつのまとまりとして生きるために、「つながり」というものを頭と体の双方で理解し感じながら、絶妙に

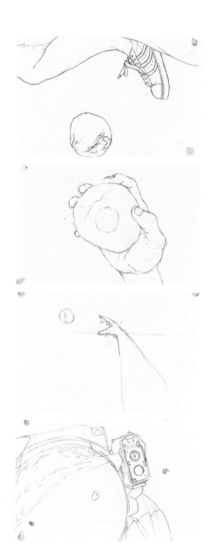

Ken: It's interesting to see this work at this point in time, because it feels like a precursor to our virtual Zoom world. When I teach, this is normal now, with students in Taiwan, Japan, Los Angeles, and Texas coming together through different screens. Maybe you were foretelling our current reality! The balance between virtual and physical connections seems to be really important here. I said earlier that real physical connections will become more important after the pandemic, but there always seems to be a fine balance between the way we bring these worlds together, understanding connections in our minds as well as through our bodies. I think your work in Mexico reflects this balance.

Tsubasa: Speaking of Mexico, that reminds me of another work I did about virtual connections, *Listen to the Same Wall* (2015).

　While in Mexico City, I had three musicians sit in three adjacent patios and play a piece of music together. But between each of them is a wall, about 10 meters high, so not only can they not see each other, they can barely hear each other. They have to guess the timing about when to start playing and when to stop. Only me and the viewers of the video, who are positioned looking

Can You Hear Me? (スケッチ) 2015

両者のバランスを取っているように思うんです。翼さんのメキシコでの作品はこのバランスをうまく捉えていますよね？

翼：そうそう、僕もいま思い出してたんですよ。バーチャルな接続をテーマにしたもうひとつの作品、《**Listen to the Same Wall**》を。

　メキシコシティの隣接する3つのパティオ（中庭）で3人のミュージシャンに曲を演奏してもらっているんですが、各々のあいだには10mほどの高い壁があって互いの姿は見えないし、その音もほとんど聞こえない。だから彼らは壁の向こう側を想像しながら自分のタイミングで演奏を始め、終えるしかありません。でもそれを上から俯瞰している僕＝鑑賞者だけは、その演奏が合っているかどうかを言うことができる。ただ、だからといって鑑賞者がそのつながりを十全に感知しているかといえば、逆に僕らは演奏者が感じている壁（あるいは隔たり）の物質性を実感できていないので、実は鑑賞者と演奏者のあいだにも「壁」があるわけです。

Listen to the Same Wall 制作中メキシコシティにて

ケン：言葉によるコミュニケーションもつながりを築いたり壁を乗り越えたりするための重要なツールなので、ちょっと言語についても話しましょうか。翼さんは日本語を母語としていますが英語も堪能で、ときに共通の第二言語のように用いて様々な文化間を渡り歩いてきましたよね。だから、どこでプロジェクトに取りかかったとしても、自分が何を目指して何をしようとしているのかを伝えるのにたいして苦労しない。そこがアメリカだろうと、香港やメキシコだろうと、コミュニケーションをとっていろんなつながりを作れるんですよね。

翼：初めてスタンディングロックに行ったとき（2013年）は全然英語ができなくて、でも不思議なことにそれでも制作を手伝ってくれるんですよね。そこがとても興味深いポイントで、たとえば説明がうまくなればなるほどうまくいかないこともあるのかなって思うんです（笑）。《**Boarding School**》の際の音源を聞き直してみると、僕と地元の人たちと、その場で理解できている内容は互いに20〜25%くらいだろうなっていうコミュニケーションしていて。でもお互いにすべてをわかりきっ

down at them from above, can tell if their playing is synched or not. But that doesn't mean we can fully share the experience of the connection between the performers, since we don't experience the wall (the distance, the lack of connection) in the physical way they do. In other words, there's also a kind of "wall" between us, as viewers/listeners, and the performers.

Ken: Perhaps we can talk a bit about language, since verbal communication is also an important element in creating connections and transcending walls. You're a native Japanese speaker, but you are also fluent in English, which provides a means to bridge many cultures—sometimes as a mutual second language. So, regardless of where you do a project, you really don't have much trouble getting across to people what it is you're trying to accomplish. Whether it's the US or Hong Kong or Mexico, you're able to communicate and create connections of different sorts.

Tsubasa: When I first went to Standing Rock in 2013, my English stunk. But strangely enough, people still helped me out. Ironically, sometimes explaining something better leads to a worse outcome! Going back and listening to the original audio for **Boarding School**, the locals and I probably only understand 20 or 25 percent of what we're saying to one another. The performance succeeded not because we understood each other completely, but because we didn't understand most of what was said and were instead forced to use our imagination to try to figure out the rest and get through it. I think that's an important feature of most of my projects, whether it be the "pull and raise" series or something else.

Ken: In other words, communication is not just about language. It can be about music or tonalities of sound, bodily movement, and shared physical experiences. It's expressly because communication passes through all sorts of means that connections are created.

Tsubasa: When I started my "pull and topple" performances in Tokyo, I didn't foresee being able to develop the series outside of Japan. I think one of the reasons physicality is emphasized in that series has to do with language and communication. "I'm not sure what this guy is trying to say to me, but I'll give him a hand anyway." That scenario becomes possible precisely because using one's body and face-to-face interactions are central to the performances. It creates this intuitive common ground. Creating networks through those kind of primitive sensibilities is an important feature of my performances. That's also why I've foregrounded language in some of works.

One I did in 2014 is even called **They Do Not Understand Each Other** (in Japanese, *literally My Words Don't Communicate*). Roughly halfway between the Japanese archipelago and the Korean Peninsula is an island called "Tsushima" in Japanese and "Daemado" in Korean. Though it's technically in Nagasaki prefecture and thus part of Japan, it's on the border with South Korea and you can get there by ferry from either Fukuoka or Busan. Tsushima has served important

Listen to the Same Wall 2015

て合意するから物事が進み出すんじゃなくて、半分以下もわからない状態だけど「こういうことなんじゃないか」っていう想像力の余白があるからこそ、それを梃子にして進められる気がするんですよね。それは「引き倒し・引き興し」にしろ他のプロジェクトにしろ、重要なポイントです。

ケン：つまり、コミュニケーションって言葉だけじゃない。音や声色、身体の動きとか、フィジカルな体験を共有することで伝わるものなんですよね。こういったいろんな媒体を通しての疎通があるからこそ、つながりが生まれるわけです。

翼：東京で始めた「引き倒し」はもともと海外展開を想定していたわけじゃなかったんですが、その一連の中でフィジカリティに重きが置かれていることの理由のひとつには、この言語／コミュニケーションの問題があるかもしれないですね。やはり身体性・対面性がプロジェクトの重要な位置を占めることで、「この人が言ってることはよくわかんないんだけど、まあ、とりあえず手伝ってあげよう」ってなりますから（笑）。でもそこには少なくとも感覚的な共通性があるってことですね。そういうプリミティブな感覚を介してつながっていくネットワークは、僕のプロジェクトでもパフォーマンスでも大事な要素になっています。そんなわけで僕には言語そのものをテーマにした作品が結構あるんですが、そのひとつがこれです。

まさに《言葉が通じない》というタイトル（笑）。日本列島と朝鮮半島のちょうど中間に、それぞれから「対馬／テマド」と呼ばれる島があります。福岡からも釜山（プサン）からもフェリーで行ける国境の島（長崎県に属する）で、過去には軍事的な防波堤になり、ナショナリストたちが互いに領有権を主張し合ってきた島でもある。その対馬で、僕は初めて会う韓国人（釜山から船で来てもらいました）の男性と落ち合って、カヌーで一緒に近くの無人島に向かいます。まさしく「月へ行く」みたいにして（笑）。そこで大きな QR コードの描かれたポールを共同作業で打ち立てるんですが、僕は韓国語がまったくわからないし、彼も日本語が全然話せない。

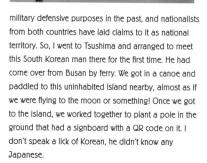

military defensive purposes in the past, and nationalists from both countries have laid claims to it as national territory. So, I went to Tsushima and arranged to meet this South Korean man there for the first time. He had come over from Busan by ferry. We got in a canoe and paddled to this uninhabited island nearby, almost as if we were flying to the moon or something! Once we got to the island, we worked together to plant a pole in the ground that had a signboard with a QR code on it. I don't speak a lick of Korean, he didn't know any Japanese.

The gallery installation version is designed to suggest that two people can get something done even if they are separated by language. There's a panel made out of driftwood. On the front is a photograph of two men, one riding on the other's shoulders, hammering a pole

言葉が通じない／*They Do Not Understand Each Other* 2014

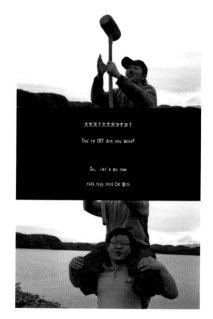

そういう言語の障壁があるなかでなんとか同じ行為を共有していく過程を表現するために、インスタレーションも工夫しました。流木を組み合わせたパネルの表には、孤島で肩車する男性 2 人がポールを打ちつけている写真。裏には、その作業中

の２人が会話になってない会話をしている映像。前者だけだと島らしき場所であることはわかるけれど２人の言葉が通じているかどうかはわからず、後者だけだと２人が通じていないことはわかるけれど場所がどこなのかがわからない。最後に、そのQRコードを携帯でスキャンするとGoogleマップ上にピンが刺さった対馬の地図が現れる。つまりこの３つの展示物それぞれは情報が少しずつ欠落していて、それを鑑賞者が組み合わせることではじめて作品のコンテクストが明らかになるという展示構造になっています。

ケン：このプロジェクトは私たちが目の前の世界を知的に理解するときのギャップに触れていて、ものすごく説得力があると思います。日本語と韓国語は文法的には近いけれど、だからといって実際に言語的な意思疎通が成立するわけではない。そこで登場するのがQRコードというグラフィックで、コンピューターという仮想空間上でコミュニケーションを媒介する中立的なリンクとして機能します。つまりこの作品は、私たちはすでに同時に複数の「言語」を生きている、という根本的な真実について語っているのです。

結集したエネルギーはどこに行くのか

翼：それで、最後に、作品の見せ方というか今回の展覧会のインスタレーションの話をしたいんですが、その前に、身体性と関わるのであらためて「引き倒し・引き興し」について補足します。
「引き倒し」のいちばん最初のモチーフは、僕のアパートでした。当時それまで10年ほど友人たちと住んでいた部屋を正確に採寸して同じサイズで立体物を作り、コピー＆ペーストするみたいに公共空間に再現しようと企てました。でも部屋のパーツが大きすぎて、なかなか一人では作れないんです。結果、同居人たちに協力してもらって完成したんですが、そのときに、プライベートな空間はひとつの質量

凹凸01 2007

into the ground on an isolated island. On the back is a video of them talking to one another but failing to communicate. With the front, you can see that they're on an island, but you can't tell that they speak different languages. With the back, you can tell that they're having difficulty communicating, but you can't see that they're on an island. If you scan the QR code with your phone, it opens Google Maps with a pin dropped on Tsushima. These three elements—the front and back of the panel and the QR code—are each incomplete as information in themselves. It's up to the viewer to put them together to figure out the context of the work.

Ken: I find this project to be profoundly compelling, as it touches upon the gaps between our phenomenological and intellectual understandings of the world. Though Japanese and Korean are related grammatically, that doesn't mean there will be actual linguistic communication between them. The QR code is introduced as another graphic, a computer code that serves as a neutral link. This work speaks to a fundamental truth of how we live within the simultaneity of multiple languages.

Where Does the Accumulated Energy Go?

Tsubasa: I was hoping we could talk a bit about the installation at the Tokyo Opera City Art Gallery. But first, I want to add a couple of things about my "pull and raise/topple" projects and the issue of physicality.

The first subject of "pull and topple" was my own apartment. I had been living in the same place, sharing it with a few other people, for about ten years. The idea was to measure our apartment carefully and make a structure the same size, recreate it in public space, like copying and pasting in a computer program. But when I got around to actually building it, the different components of the room were too big to handle by myself, so I had my roommates help me finish it. That's when I had this realization that a private space has a mass. Nothing could be more private than my own room, yet because of its size I wasn't able to recreate it by myself, I needed to get together a team to help me. Then I thought, what if that process itself was the goal? That's where the idea of pulling ropes together to conquer the mass of a structure came from.

In other words, because the mass and gravity of the structures are important, "pull and raise/topple" is essentially about the conversion of energy. The greater the mass of a structure, the greater human power required to move it, and the greater number of people

を持っている、というアイデアが浮かびました。つまり、自分の部屋というごく私的な空間でさえ重くて作れないというハードルが、協力してくれる人たちを集めてチームを作り、制作へのプロセスを生み出してくれる。だとすれば、そのハードル自体をゴールとして設定したら面白いんじゃないか。その重さの克服として、構築物を集合的にロープで引き倒すという「引き倒し」のパフォーマンスが生まれていったんです。

　要は構築物の質量と重力が「引き倒し・引き興し」の重要な要素なんですが、そこにはエネルギーの換算が生じると思うんです。構築物の質量が大きくなればなるほど人を必要とし、実際に人が集まってくるんですが、たとえば街中の人通りの多い場所では構築物を動かすというゴールが簡単になってしまうので、逆に構築物のほうを大きくする。僕が興味を持っているのは、それを作品として展示する際、「引き倒し・引き興し」を達成するために結集したエネルギーはいったいどこにいったのか？　そのエネルギーは場所を変えてどのように変換されうるのか？ということなんです。

　質量として残された構築物をそのパフォーマンス映像とともに会場に展示したときに、それがかつてのエネルギーをどんなふうに物語るのか注目してるんですが、ひとつ言えるのは、そのエネルギーの行き先や変換に、僕たちの体験＝記憶と記録

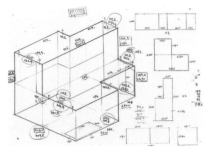

who will come together to help achieve that. Since it's easier to find people to help in places where there are more people around, I make the structure bigger in places that have more people. But where does the energy that was accumulated to pull and raise or topple go when you display the work in a gallery? How does the energy change when the location changes? That's a question I'm interested in.

When you display the structure (the leftover mass) and a video of the performance in a gallery, how does that ensemble communicate the energy that was part of the performance? That's something I pay attention to. Where that energy goes, or what it turns into, has a lot to do with the problem of how we, as participants or

Turningman 2012/2021

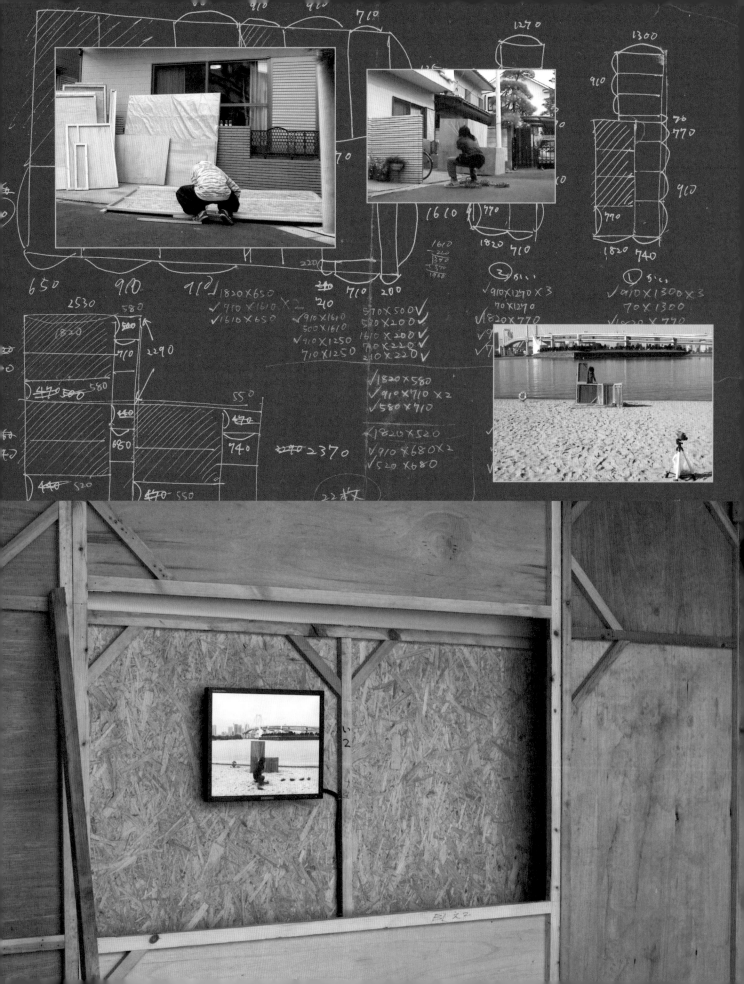

凹凸01　2007
自分の部屋の間取りを2.5分の1スケールで制作し、実家の前で母親と引き倒した。

のジレンマが深く関わっていることです。会場に展示するのは各プロジェクトの構築物と映像と写真、つまり行為のドキュメントですよね。しかしそれらの記録をバランスよく構成しても、実際のパフォーマンスで生じたエネルギーとはどこまでいっても一緒にはならない。だから両者を別々のものとして捉えるんですが、構成の仕方によってはあのときの現場でのエネルギーを別のかたちで還元できるんじゃないか、そう考えて今回のインスタレーションに挑戦しているわけです。そうした展示構成と空間設計はまさに建築に関わることなので、ケンさんの意見を聞いてみたいです。

　先にインスタレーションの説明をすると、今回の展示会場、オペラシティアートギャラリーの空間は大きく3つに分かれています。そこで、各空間の広がりをある種ストーリーを配置する「尺」に見立てて展示を構成しました。たとえば映画なら2時間ある尺の中でストーリーが展開されていくように。このギャラリーは運が良いことに鑑賞者が巡回できる構造になっていて、うまくやれば永久にループを作れる。なので今回僕はこの構造を利用して、展示も円環的になるよう設計しています。インスタレーションというのは常に空間に制約を受けながら構成され展開されるものだと思うんですけど、循環する構造を空間が持つことで鑑賞者が繰り返し作品を体験したり、同じ美術館に多くの人が繰り返し訪れたりというような、循環と反復について、また、そもそも建築空間とそこを訪れる者との時間の関係について、どのように考えますか？

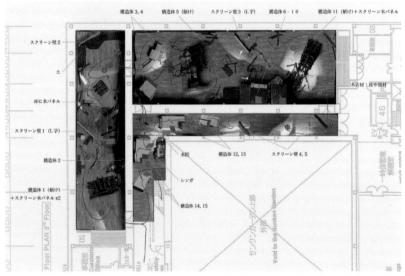

「縄張りと島」展示プラン　Turf and Perimeter (plan)

ケン：この展示構成の図面を見て、磯崎新の「**MA, Space-Time in Japan**」展（1978～1979年）を思い出しました。空間と時間が見事に融合していて、両者のつながりがよく理解できる展覧会でした。鑑賞者はそれぞれ、時空間に対する自身の主観に応じて展示と向き合います。だから翼さんのインスタレーションも、上映時間や座席が固定された映画館で見る映画というよりは、個人が自由にそれらを変えたり調節できるオンデマンドムービーに近い。2017年に無人島プロダクションで開催された翼さんの展示「**(Drawing) Fractions of the Longest Distance [Mexico City ⇄ Jakarta]**」も思い出すんですが、そこでは作品映像をただ投影するだけでなく、その素材や構

viewers, experience things or remember and document them. What's displayed in the gallery is documentation–the objects, videos, and photographs of each project. No matter how carefully you arrange those pieces of documentation, it will never have the same energy as the actual performance. You have to take that ensemble as something different. But still I wonder if there's a way to recover some of that original energy and present it in a new way. That was one of the challenges for the current exhibition. Since exhibition design and spatial layout is ultimately an architectural question, I was curious to hear your thoughts on the subject.

Just to provide a basic overview, the exhibition at Tokyo Opera City Art Gallery is divided spatially into three general sections. Each section is paced and laid out to tell a story, like with a movie, where you have to tell a story in the course of, say, two hours. Luckily, the galleries at Tokyo Opera City Art Gallery are designed in a way that visitors can circle back through the exhibition if they wish to, in an infinite loop potentially. So, I decided to design the exhibition likewise in the shape of a loop. Installations typically have to work with the preexisting limitations of the space they occupy and structure the narrative accordingly. But what if that space allows for circulation and for visitors to return and reexperience the exhibition, and for many people to do the same inside a single museum? I'd be curious to know your thoughts on the subject of circulation and repetition with regards to architectural space, and how people in such spaces experience time.

Ken: In looking at the plan of your exhibition, I recall Isozaki Arata's exhibition *MA, Space-Time*, which really relies on the fusion of space and time to understand these connections. The viewer individually engages the exhibition according to this subjectivity of space-time. So, rather than a movie in a theater that is fixed, your installation is more like an on-demand movie which the individual can freely interact with. I remember the installation of your show *Fractions of the Longest Distance [Mexico City ⇄ Jakarta]* at MUJIN-TO Production in 2017, where it was not just video projections and monitors but an attempt to recreate the events physically by exhibiting the materials and the built structures at their original scale.

At Tokyo Opera City Art Gallery, in terms of architecture, you have three rooms, though the layout enables a highly personal and subjective experience in terms of how you perceive scale and the impact of scale within the gallery space, which is in contrast to the vastness or compression of the performance sites, whether that be the plains of Standing Rock or the tunnels of Hong Kong. In an indoor space, even when things are the same size, they're experienced differently than when they are out in the open. So, the juxtaposition your installation creates of looking at faraway, open spaces within an enclosed context offers a unique perspective upon each of your projects. It transforms your work further. I think each room will be like each act or performance, distinct in shape. But when and how each visitor experiences them will be key to the overall effect.

(Drawing) Fractions of the Longest Distance [Mexico City ⇄ Jakarta] (展示風景) 2017

(Drawing) Fractions of the Longest Distance [Mexico City ⇄ Jakarta] (展示風景) 2017

築物も実際のスケールで展示することで作品の体験を物理的に再構築していました。

　建築ということでいえば、東京オペラシティアートギャラリーには大きく3つの部屋がありますが、この展示空間内部の規模感やそのインパクトを鑑賞者がどのように受け取るかによって、非常に個人的で主観的な経験をすることも可能になります。それは、スタンディングロックの平原や香港の地下通路といった、実際のパフォーマンス現場の広大な景色や閉塞的な空間とは対照的ですね。たとえ物が同じサイズでも、室内と屋外とではその経験も違ってきます。そのため、閉ざされた環境の中でもはるか遠くまで見晴らすような視点の並置を作り出す今回の翼さんの展示は、過去の個々のプロジェクトにまた別の新たな見方を与え、作品をさらに変質させるでしょう。さながら各部屋がそれぞれ固有の姿形を持つ、劇の一幕でありパフォーマンスのようです。けれど、訪問者がいつどのようにしてそれを体験するかによって全体の印象はまったく変わってきます。

翼：やはり「体験」という言葉が出てきちゃいますか（笑）。体験というのは視点と密接に絡み合っていて、今回の展示では、その視点をどうずらしていけるかを考えて展示しています。部屋を区切って次の展開を作ったりする、展覧会ではお馴染みのパーテーションを今回は使わないと最初から決めていて、その理由のひとつは「音」です。

　今回のインスタレーションの核になるのは、スタンディングロックとか福島とかマレーシアとか香港とか、違う時間に違う場所にいる人たちとのコネクションとディスコネクションを会場の東京オペラシティアートギャラリーから同時に発見することなんですが、その視点の〝ずれ〟を作るために真っ先に取り組んだのが、音なんですよね。だから、矛盾かもしれないけれど、音が重要な要素になっている《**Woodstock 2017**》や《**Underground Orchestra**》や《**Listen to the Same Wall**》といった作品の配置をまず考えて、そのあいだをなるべくパーテーションで区切らないようにしました。なぜかといえば映画と同じで、鑑賞者は作品を一人で見ると同時にみんなとも見るからなんですよね。作品に没入している鑑賞者はふつう他の鑑賞者の存在を意識してはいないんだけれど、見渡せる空間とそこで共有する音を強調することによって、そこにいる他者としての鑑賞者を意識させることができる。そして、その鑑賞者同士の視点のずれを、映像内のプロジェクト参加者たちとの視点のずれにつなげていくイメージで、それをアンプで増幅させるように音のストーリー展開を考えて会場を構成しているんです。

　音のために設計される建物もたくさんあるくらい、建築は音とも密接に関わり合っていると思うんですが、建築と音との関係についてはどう思いますか？

ケン：音は床や壁、そして空間の構造によって反射したり屈折したりするので、立つ位置によってその体験も異なります。そのとき建築はランドスケープへと変化し、歩いて通ることのできる庭にもなる。日本庭園における「見え隠れ」という経験的な概念をここで思い出しますが、最後に何があるのかは初めはわからないけれど、空間を移動していくことによって徐々に明らかになっていくプロセスのことですね。ここにもまた、物理的な次元と比喩的な次元とがあります。歴史的な時間の中ではすべてはとても複雑に絡み合っていて、私たちはどこに向かっているのかわからな

Tsubasa: I figured the word "experience" would come up eventually! Experience, of course, is intimately related to perspective. For the current show, I wanted to try to displace the visitor's perspective. From the beginning, I decided not to do what a lot of shows do, which is subdivide the rooms with partitions and control the narrative that way. I wanted to use "sound" in that way instead.

　A central feature of the Tokyo Opera City Art Gallery installation is allowing visitors to explore the connections and disconnections between the different times and different places represented in the works, whether it be Standing Rock, Fukushima, Malaysia, or Hong Kong—and not just separately, but all at once. To induce that displacement of perspective, I've relied most of all on sound. This might seem counterintuitive, but the works whose position I first decided were those in which sound is paramount—like **Woodstock 2017**, **Underground Orchestra**, and **Listen to the Same Wall**. I minimized the partitions between them as much as I could. The idea was that, like with movies, people experience artworks in a gallery simultaneously alone and among other people. If someone is focused on a work, usually they're unconscious of other visitors around them. But by having an open space where both the eye and sound can move across it, each visitor becomes more conscious of other people in that space. Furthermore, the gap between different viewers' perspectives is echoed by the gap between different performers' perspectives in the videos. To amplify that effect, I took care to design the exhibition around the stories that sounds tell.

　I know that many buildings are designed with sound in mind, but do you have any thoughts about the relationship between sound and architecture?
Ken: Since sound is reflected and refracted by the floors and walls and the proportions of the space, the experience of it is different in different locations. Architecture changes into a landscape as well as a garden that you move through. I am recalling the

い。だからこそ、建築的空間も芸術的空間になりうるのです。知ってのとおり、空間（展示空間も含めて）は目で視覚的に捉えることもできますが、身体を通して体感することもできます。建築理論家のユハニ・パルラスマが「皮膚にある眼」と呼んだように、空間は目で見なくとも体験できるのです。あなたの作品を体験するとき、それがどのように作用するのか、どんなコミュニケーションの形態をとるのか、とても気になります。翼さんは自分の作品が視覚的に見られることは必須だと思いますか？　それとも身体を介して別のかたちで体験できると思いますか？

翼：目も身体の一部なのでインターフェースとしては重要なんですけど、たしかに展示空間の持っている情報は目だけでは捉えきれないほど多様ですよね。もちろん音もあれば、隣の鑑賞者との距離や温度といった様々な要素がある。それは体験の質の違いでもあって、音の体験を強く記憶する人もいれば、匂いを記憶する人もいる。どの高さから見るか、どんな人たちと見るかによっても、体験の質は変わってくる。そういう体験のディテールってすごく断片的で、刹那的な記憶を植えつけると思うんですよね。

　引き倒しの場合、構築物の自重もあって、動きだしてから地面に着落するまで1秒もなかったりするんですが、参加した人たちはそれぞれその体験をまったく違った視点で共有していて、そんな極小的で刹那的な記憶を拡大解釈して人に伝えたりもするし、別の角度から別の物語として伝えたりもしますよね。いずれにせよ、訴えるのが聴覚であれ視覚であれ触覚であれ、僕は「断片的な記憶」というのをひとつのキーワードとして意識的に映像を作っています。ループする映像作品だと鑑賞者は自分で見始めるポイントを決められないので、どこから見ても各自の体験に結びつくように。今回の展示で、1回目、2回目、3回目……と空間を巡回するごとに、作品やそれを見ている人たちとの距離に新たな変化が生まれていけば、いまことは別の場所で行なわれたプロジェクトの断片的な記憶が鑑賞者の中で形を変えて、今回の展示の体験へとすり替わってくれるんじゃないかなと期待しています。

（2021年6月、Zoom で東京とシアトルをつなぎ対談を収録）

experiential notion of "hide and reveal" (*mie kakure*) in Japanese gardens, where things are gradually revealed through the process of moving through space, though it's not apparent from the beginning what unfolds at the end. Again, there's something physical and also metaphorical. In historical time, we don't know where we're going, though it's all connected in complex ways. Architectural space can thus also become an artistic space. As you know, space (including the space of an exhibition) can be perceived visually through the eyes, but also physically through the body. Architectural theorist Juhani Pallasmaa has described this as "the eyes of the skin." You can experience space even without seeing it, as if your were blind. I wonder how that might play out in an experience of your projects, how that might be communicated. I wonder if it's always necessary to see your work visually, or if could it be experienced through the body in a different way?

Tsubasa: Since eyes are part of the body, the interface between the two is important. But you're right that information arranged physically in an exhibition space is plural enough that it cannot be consumed by vision alone. There's also sound, and the proximity or warmth of other visitors standing next to you. All of that impacts the quality of experience, especially since one person might experience things more strongly through sound, while another might do so through smell. Or depending on what height you're viewing the work from, or who you're with at the gallery. The details of experience are extremely fragmentary and can seed highly ephemeral memories.

　With my pulling and toppling performances, because of the weight, once you get a structure moving, it might not be more than a second before it falls and crashes to the ground. Nonetheless, each participant might have a totally different experience of the same event. When the memory of that experience is narrated to other people, its smallness becomes larger and its ephemerality more fixed, resulting in different stories based on different perspectives. Whether it's hearing or seeing or touching, the idea of "fragmentary memories" is something I'm very conscious of when composing the videos. With videos on a loop, viewers can't decide at what point they're going to start watching from, so they have to put together the experiences they witness as they happen to come. If a visitor passes through the exhibition once, twice, or three times, each iteration will introduce new changes in how they relate to the works. The fragmentary memories of a project that was made in a different place and time take different forms inside the visitor. They quietly become the visitor's memories of the experience of the exhibition instead. That, at least, is my hope.

(June 2021, between Tokyo and Seattle by Zoom)

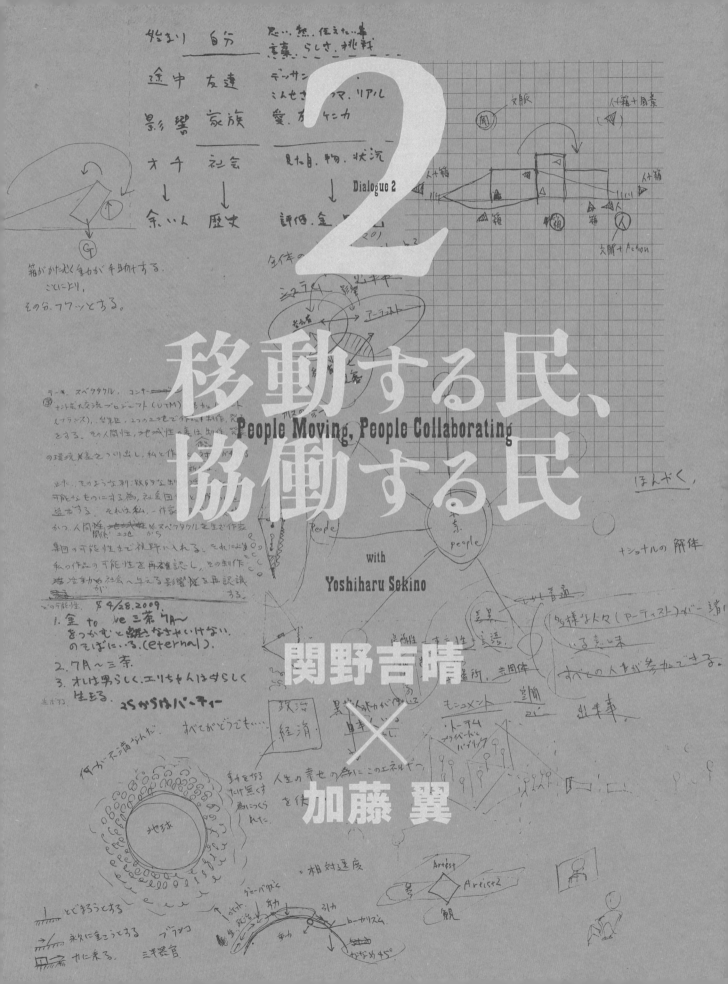

2

Dialogue 2

移動する民、協働する民

People Moving, People Collaborating

with

Yoshiharu Sekino

関野吉晴 × 加藤 翼

関野吉晴（せきの・よしはる）

探検家、医師、武蔵野美術大学名誉教授（文化人類学）。1949年東京都生まれ。一橋大学在学中に同大探検部を創設し、1971年にアマゾン川全域を踏査。1993年、ホモサピエンス発祥の地アフリカからアメリカ大陸まで人類が拡散していった行程を自らの脚力と腕力だけをたよりに遡行する「グレートジャーニー」を開始。南米最南端のナバリーノ島をカヤックで出発し、2002年にタンザニア・ラエトリに終着。2004年には日本に人類が到来した3つのルートを辿る「新グレートジャーニー」に出発（2011年にゴール）。植村直己冒険賞受賞（1999年）。著書に『グレートジャーニー』シリーズ（角川文庫）、『地球ものがたり』シリーズ（ほるぷ出版）など多数。いまも探検家として世界各地への旅を続けている。

Yoshiharu Sekino   Adventurer, doctor, and Professor Emeritus at Musashino Art University (Cultural Anthropology). Born in Tokyo in 1949. Created the Explorer's Club while a student at Hitotsubashi University. Traveled the length of the Amazon River in 1971. In 1993, began "The Great Journey," tracing in reverse the passage of homo sapiens from their birthplace in Africa to their migration to the Americas, relying solely upon on the strength of his own arms and legs. He set off from Navarino Island at the southern tip of South America, crossed the Atlantic Ocean, then proceeded on foot across Africa to Laetoli in Tanzania. In 2004, began "The New Great Journey," tracing the three routes by which humans arrived in the Japanese archipelago, finishing in 2011. In 1999, received the Uemura Naomi Adventure Prize. Among his books in Japanese are *The Great Journey* series (KADOKAWA) and *the Tales of the Earth* series (Holp Shuppan). He continues to explore the planet today.

　移 動 す る 民、 協 働 す る 民

関野吉晴　✕　加藤翼

Dialogue 02
**People Moving,
People Collaborating**
with Yoshiharu Sekino

翼：探検家・武蔵野美術大学名誉教授で医師でもある関野吉晴さんとのつながりは、僕が武蔵野美術大学に在学していた2003〜2007年にちょうど教壇に立っていらして文化人類学演習を受講したのがきっかけで、大学を卒業した翌年の2008年、関野さんの「新グレートジャーニー」の途中、インドネシアで船を作るプロジェクトに参加させてもらったんです。「グレートジャーニー」というのは、およそ700万年前にアフリカで誕生し、南アメリカ大陸の最南端にまで到達した人類5万3000kmの旅路を逆ルートで辿るという、関野さんの一大探険プロジェクトです（1993〜2002年）。「新グレートジャーニー」（2004〜2011年）のほうは、その人類がいつどのようにして日本列島にやって来たのか、その主要ルート（シベリアからサハリンを経由する北方ルート、朝鮮半島ルート、インドネシアから海を渡るルート）を辿る旅路でした。

Tsubasa: I first met Yoshiharu Sekino, an explorer, doctor, and Professor Emeritus at Musashino Art University, when I was a student at the same university between 2003 and 2007 and attended his cultural anthropology lectures. In 2008, the year after I graduated, I took part in the boat-building project in Indonesia he organized as part of his *The New Great Journey*. The first iteration, *The Great Journey* (1993-2002), traced in reverse the 53,000-kilometer journey of homo sapiens from their birthplace in Africa some 7 million years ago to the southern tip of South America. *The New Great Journey* (2004-11) traced the three main routes by which humans arrived into the Japanese archipelago: the northern route through Siberia and Sakhalin, the Korean Peninsula route, and the sea route from Indonesia.

　インドネシアではリサーチも兼ねて方々を回っていたんですが、バリ島の東のほうにあるレンバタ島のラマレラ村で初めてクジラ漁を目の当たりにしました。もともとクジラ漁が盛んな村として知られていますが、実際は漁というよりは狩猟のようでした。10人くらいずつ乗った25隻のボートの群れで沖に出て、ラマファーと呼ばれる射手が巨大な銛をクジラに突き刺すんですが、そのボートが手に負えないと合図を出すと、周りで見守っていたボートも加わって最終的には集団でクジラを仕留めていく。その漁に僕らが立ち会ったとき、獲ったクジラが村の一角にある岩礁に引っかかってしまって、そのクジラを村の人たち総出でロープで引っ張り出そうとする場面がありました。巨大で重すぎてビクともしないクジラをなんとか動かそうと村の人たちが人数を増やしながら協力していく風景が、ラマレラの集団的な狩猟のあり方をよく表わしていて、「引っ張る」という行為への僕のある種の原風

In our research travels around Indonesia, we went east of Bali to the island of Lembata. There, in the village of Lamalera, I saw people whaling for the first time. Lamalera is famous for whaling, which is more like hunting than it is fishing. A group of about 25 boats, each with about ten people on it, go out to sea. The harpooners are called lamafas, and they use these giant harpoons to spear the whales. If one boat can't kill a whale themselves, they signal to the other boats to join them and finish off their prey as a group. On the day that we arrived, a whale they killed had gotten stuck on some rocks on the edge of the village. The villagers were desperately trying to pull it in with ropes, but it wouldn't move. Watching more and more people arrive to help move this massive animal, you really got a feel

景として、その場面を撮影した記録映像《**Haul the Whale First**》を今回の展覧会にも登場させています。

　まだ僕が「アーティスト」になる前、そのときに見た集団的な狩猟のあり方やコミュニティとの関係性、クジラという、一人の人間の手には負えない巨大なものと対峙することで生まれる原初的な共同作業とチームワークは、大きな構築物にロープをかけて地元民たちと一緒に引っ張る僕の「引き倒し・引き興し」という作品群にも通じていると思います。いわば現在の僕にまでいたる端緒を関野さんとともに経験させてもらったのが幸運だと思っていて、今回こうして文化人類学的視点から作品についてお話ししてみたいと思いました。

for the culture of collective hunting in Lamalera. As this event was also one of the original inspirations behind my interest in "pulling," I decided to include a video, *Haul the Whale First*, which we shot that day in my exhibition at Tokyo Opera City Art Gallery.

Though our trip to Lamalera took place before I became a professional "artist," watching how the villagers hunt as a group, relationship dynamics within the community, and how being confronted with things that are too big for any one person to handle alone inspires elementary forms of collective action and teamwork—all of that had a real impact on my art and collaborating with locals to manipulate oversize structures with ropes in my "pull and raise" and "pull and topple" projects. Which is to say, if I hadn't had the good fortune of experiencing what I did with you in Indonesia, Professor Sekino, I wouldn't be who I am today. That's why I was hoping we might talk about my work from the perspective of your field, cultural anthropology.

"Turf" and "Perimeter"

Tsubasa: So, the title of my exhibition at Tokyo Opera City Art Gallery is *Turf and Perimeter*, or *Nawabari to Shima* in Japanese. Though "nawabari" literally refers to a roped-off area and "shima" is the word for island, they can also both be translated as "territory." However, "territory" encompasses a lot more than just the delimited turf implied by "nawabari." It can also be the land and water controlled by a nation or the habitat of an animal species. My work as an artist has entailed traveling to different places around the world, conducting fieldwork among the local community, then executing a project with their cooperation, and finally presenting documentation of the project within a gallery setting. My movement between communities is basically a movement between territories, hence the title of the current exhibition. Professor Sekino, since your work has taken you to communities around the world, I was wondering what your thoughts are about the relationship between elementary forms of collective action and the formation of communities.

「縄張り」と「島」

翼：では最初に、「**縄張りと島（Turf and Perimeter）**」というのが、東京オペラシティアートギャラリーで開催される僕の展覧会のタイトルです。文字通りには、縄で囲まれるか海に浮かんでいるかの違いはあれ、「縄張り」も「島（シマ）」も両方「テリトリー」という言葉に翻訳可能なんですが、「テリトリー」という言葉には「縄張り」以外にもいろんな意味が含まれます。領土とか、版図とか、生態とか。僕自身は世界の土地土地のコミュニティに入ってリサーチを重ね、地元の人々の協力を得ながらプロジェクトを起こしてはそれを展覧会として記録するということを、場所を移動しながら繰り返してきました。そのコミュニティ間の移動、つまり「テリトリーからテリトリーへ」の運動を「縄張りと島」と意訳したんです。関野さんこそ世界各地のあらゆるコミュニティのあいだを移動してきたわけですが、原初的な共同作業とコミュニティの生成とのあいだにはどんな関係があると思いますか？

関野：まず「縄張りと島」っていうタイトルが面白いよね。人類の700万年の歴史の中でその99％が採集や狩猟をして暮らしていて、農耕を始めたのはたかだか今から1万年前だった。狩猟採集民は何年かごとに移動するので、そもそも自分たち

のテリトリーってないんだよね。対して、定住する農耕民は土地がいちばん大事で離れない。「土地を売る」っていう概念が生まれたのも、感染症の世界規模の流行も、農耕が始まってからの現象なんだ。もちろん世界中にこんなにも人類が増殖したのは農耕のおかげだけれど、それによって「格差」も生じた。狩猟採集民にとっての土地はみんなのもの、あるいは精霊とか目に見えない大きな存在のものなので、土地を巡る争いやいざこざも起こらない。今でもアラスカやシベリアで行なわれているクジラ漁もそうだけど、狩猟ではいつ食料が獲れるのかわからないし蓄えることができないので、獲物もみんなで平等に分けるのが特徴。

　ちなみに人類が肉食を始めたのは今から240万年ほど前から（人類誕生からおよそ500万年後）で、その当初はまだ狩りなんてしていなかった。ライオンやヒョウが獲物を食べ残し、それにありつくハイエナやジャッカルが食べ残したあとを、チンパンジーと人類が食べ争った。ただ、その場で独り占めして食べるチンパンジーとは違って、人間はわざわざ家族や仲間のところに持ち帰って食べた。この「平等に分ける」というのが人間のコミュニティの規範になったんだね。

翼：すると、農耕を始めたことによって人類のコミュニティの形がまったく変わったってことでしょうか？

関野：コミュニティの形はできるんだけど、その内部でさっそく格差が生まれた。たくさん収穫できるやつが食料を抱え込んで、他の多くの人が隷属するような状態がずっと続いていた。だから農耕って、とくに良いことないんだよね（笑）。

翼：でもその農耕が現在までこうして残ったわけですよね。

関野：残ったけれど決して安定していたわけじゃない。農耕の起こりは中東のチグリス・ユーフラテス川流域だとされていて、小麦を作ることができるようになった人類はヨーロッパへと移動するんだけど、その地にすぐには農耕は伝わらなかった。

Sekino: First of all, let me say that I really like the title of your exhibition. For the 7 million years of human history, 99% of that has been hunting and gathering. Farming only started about ten thousand years ago. Hunter-gatherers relocate every few years, which basically means that they don't have their own "territory." For settled agricultural communities, on the other hand, nothing is more important than land and holding on to it. The phenomenon of selling land, as well as that of global pandemics, dates to the creation of agricultural societies. That the earth's population has increased as much as it has is, of course, due to agriculture, but so is the creation of class differences. Within hunter-gatherer societies, land belongs to everyone, or to spirits or larger entities invisible to the human eye. As a result, you don't have quarrels or wars over land. Still today, with whaling in places like Alaska and Siberia, since there's no way of knowing when you'll be able to catch something again, nor is there any way to preserve what you catch, anything caught is divided equally among everyone in the community.

　Meat-eating began about 2.4 million years ago, so about 5 million years after the birth of humans. But at that point, humans still didn't hunt. They were basically scavengers, fighting with other primates, like chimpanzees, over the carcasses of animals killed by predators like lions and leopards, then picked over by hyenas and jackals. Unlike chimpanzees, which ate as much as they wanted or could for themselves on the spot, humans carried food back to their friends and

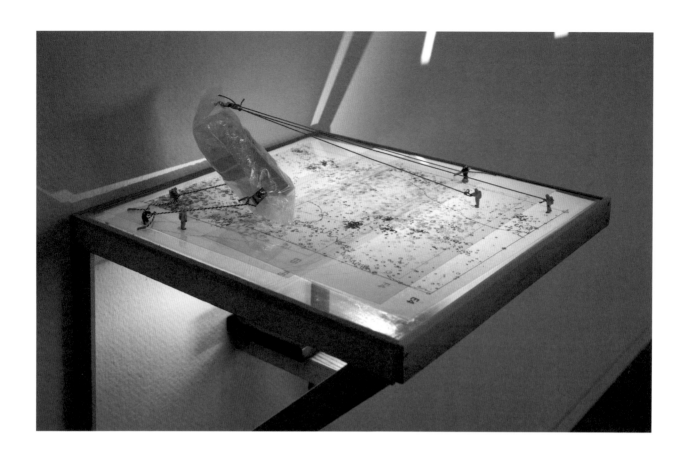

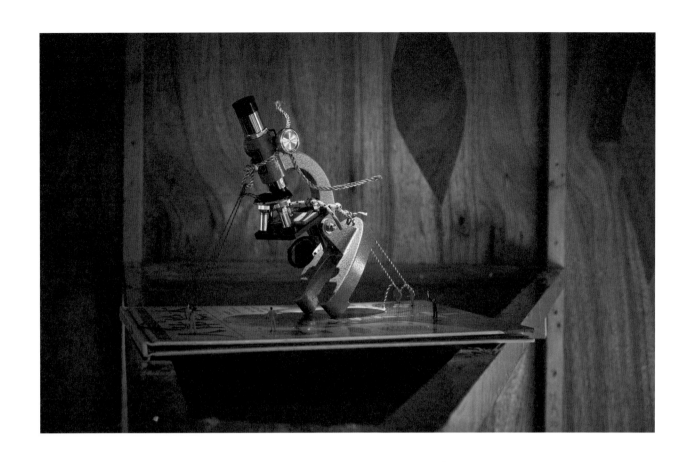

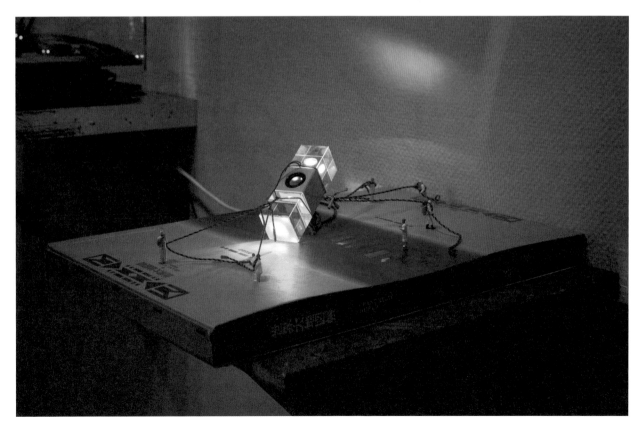

これは想像だけど、草取りや害虫・天候対策など年じゅう気を揉む農耕よりも、狩りをしているほうが面白かったんだろうね。狩りの獲物は英語で「game」と言うくらいだから楽しい。まあ、つまりは農耕によって土地は自分のものだっていう意識が芽生えるまで、縄張りやシマの意識ははるかに低かった。

翼：土地をめぐるそうした意識の問題が今でもはっきり残っているもののひとつが、僕もそこでプロジェクトを行なったことのあるネイティブアメリカンの居留地ですよね。元来は移動しながらバッファローを狩るネイティブアメリカンたちは、テントのような持ち運び式住居の

Boarding Shcool 2013

「ティピー」に住み、「スウェットロッジ」という儀式（サウナのように高温に蒸された小屋で暗闇の中、人がぎゅうぎゅう詰めになって行なう）も、僕が体験したものは場所を変えてどこでもできるような簡易なつくりになっていました。けれどその子供たちは、白人キリスト教徒の開拓者たちによって「寄宿学校（Boarding School）」に強制的に入れられてしまうわけです。そこでは部族の言語を禁止されたり、神聖なシンボルである髪を切られたりと、厳しい同化教育が行なわれていました。

Tepee Rocket 2013

関野：音楽だって舞踏だって、そこで自分たちの文化は全部根こそぎにされたわけだよね。英語をしゃべらないと殴られるし。

翼：そうですね。僕が行ったのはスー族の住むノースダコタ州のスタンディングロックという居留地で、幼少時に受けた英語教育によって自分たちの言葉はほとんど失われてしまいました。この居留地の寄宿学校が閉鎖されたのは、なんとごく最近の1985年だそうです。今ではスー族の手で居留地に建てられ運営されているシッティング・ブル大学で部族の言葉を掘り起こして辞書を作ったりと、自分たちの文化ソースを保存するクラスをやっています。

family and ate it together. This practice of "sharing things equally" became the norm within human communities.

Tsubasa: So basically, agriculture completely changed human communities?

Sekino: It created communities, but it also quickly created class hierarchies within them. Those who were able to produce a lot tended to monopolize foodstuffs, thus making the majority dependent upon them. In that sense, the development of agriculture is not inherently a good thing!

Tsubasa: But it still exists today.

Sekino: It does, though it's not necessarily stable. It is said that agriculture began along the Tigris-Euphrates river system, and from there the cultivation of wheat migrated outward with people as they moved to Europe. But otherwise, its spread wasn't as fast as you might think. This is just a theory, but rather than having to deal with the hassle of weeds, pests, and changes in the weather, as one has to with farming, hunting was probably more attractive to most people. I mean, in English, they even call hunting prey "game," that's how enjoyable it must have been to them! In any case, until agriculture instills the idea that land is owned by someone, consciousness of "territory" remained weak.

Tsubasa: One place you can still see the legacy of that tension clearly is on Native American reservations, where I've done a few projects. Traditionally, Plains Indians migrated while hunting buffalo, so they had these portable, tent-like dwellings called "tepees." There's also something called a "sweat lodge," used for a ceremony in which people cram into a hut that is dark and made hot and steamy inside like a sauna. Those lodges, too, at least the one I went inside, are made such that you can easily move them from one place to the next. However, once White Christians arrived, they took the children of these nomadic peoples and put them into boarding schools, where they were subjected to severe assimilation policies that banned them from using their native tribal language and forced them to do things like cut their hair, which is a holy symbol to many Native American communities.

Sekino: Yes, they also banned their music and dance. The whole goal was to rip out their culture from the root. They'd even beat them if they didn't speak English.

Tsubasa: Exactly. The reservation I went to was called Standing Rock, in North Dakota. It belongs to a tribe known as the Sioux. Since most of the people there grew up educated in English, the local language is in danger of being lost. The boarding school there only closed in 1985, so pretty recently. At Sitting Bull College, which was built and is operated by the Sioux, they are creating a Sioux dictionary and trying to revive the language, as part of a larger curriculum designed to preserve the wellsprings of their culture.

コミュニティの結束力とそこから弾かれる者

翼：《**Boarding School**》もそうですが、僕の「引き倒し・引き興し」では大きな構造体を引っ張って動かすのはもちろん、構造体を制作するのも一人ではできないんです。制作そのものだけじゃなくて、構築物の素材をその土地で集めるのにも、制作の場所を確保するのにも、現地の人たちの協力が必須。こういう共同作業はこれまでの話を受けると、すごく農耕的なのかなと思ったんですけど。

関野：それは違うんじゃないかな。狩猟民だって、収穫物が一人じゃ重いから持ってくれよ、なんてことはあると思うけど。

翼：あ……そうですよね。さっき獲物は「ゲーム」だとおっしゃっていましたが、「game」の語源には「参加する」「ともにする」「人が集まる」といった意味もあるようなんです。僕のプロジェクトだと構造体をみんなで一緒に引っ張って動かすのがゴールなので、それができそうにない雰囲気になると周囲で見ていた人たちもどんどん参加してくるんですね。これも冒頭のクジラ漁の話に通じると思うんですが、コミュニティの共同作業におけるチームワークのあり方って、狩猟型と農耕型とでなにか決定的な差はあるのでしょうか？

関野：それよりも、インドネシアでのクジラ漁と翼くんの一連の「引き倒し・引き興し」とのいちばん大きな違いは、参加者同士がみんな知り合いかどうかという点じゃないかな。チームを構成する全員の名前も性格も知っている人たちが協力し合うのがクジラ漁で、「引き倒し・引き興し」はとにかく知らない者同士でも一緒にやってみようと助け合っているわけで。

翼：現地の人から見れば、僕が一番よそ者ですよね（笑）。コミュニティの外からやって来て、その土地にまつわるネガティブな歴史や、コミュニティの抱える課題やグループ間同士の軋轢といった話を聞かせてもらってフィールドワークをして、こういうものを作ってみたらいいんじゃないかと提案を繰り返して、そうやって形になった作品を中心に地元の人々と一緒にパフォーマンスする。ご指摘のとおり、それはすごく即時的なグループワークで、たとえば「引き倒し・引き興し」に参加した人同士で新しい政党を立ち上げたりはしないんですよね（笑）。とはいえ、ネイティブアメリカンの人たちやインドネシアで出会った人たちとは今でもFacebookやInstagramでつながっていて関係も続いています。
　　少し話を戻すと、2008年に関野さんのインドネシアでのプロジェクトに参加したあと、作家として作品を発表し始めてすぐ震災が起こってしまいました。当時は武蔵野美術大学の卒業制作の延長線上で、自分のアパートの間取りや家といった私的空間をトレースして作った構造体を公共空間に出現させて、それをみんなでロープで引っ張って倒したり壊したりする「引き倒し」というスタイルで作品を制作していたんですが、考え直さざるをえなくなりました。津波で家が破壊され住む場所を失った人たちや原発事故で家を追われることになってしまった人たちが何十万と

Community Solidarity and the Outcast

Tsubasa: With my "pull and raise" and "pull and topple" projects, not only are the structures unable to be pulled and moved by a single person, they also can't be built by one person. **Boarding School** was no different. I needed locals' cooperation not just to build it, but also to collect the necessary materials and secure a place where the structure could be constructed. Thinking about what you said earlier, I wonder if the collective work required for my projects is "agricultural" in a way.

Sekino: I'm not sure I would describe it that way. Even with hunters, it's easy to imagine situations requiring others' help, like if your quarry is too big and you need help carrying it.

Tsubasa: That's true. Earlier you mentioned that hunted animals are called "game" in English. Apparently, the etymology of "game" includes ideas of "participation," "communion," and "people coming together." The goal of each of my projects is to have people come together to pull and move a structure. When it looks like the structure is too big to move, or the participants too few, spectators will spontaneously join in to help, like in the whaling example I started off with. Would you say that there is a fundamental difference in collective action and teamwork between hunting societies versus agricultural societies?

Sekino: More than that, I would say that probably the biggest difference between your pulling projects and the whalers in Indonesia is whether or not everyone already knows one another. With the whalers, everyone in the team already knows everyone else's name and personality. With your projects, it's a group of strangers working together.

Tsubasa: From the locals' perspective, I'm the biggest outsider in all of my projects! I arrive from outside the community, conduct my fieldwork by asking them about negative aspects of local history, problems internal to the community, friction between its members, et cetera, then propose different ideas about what to make, until finally coming up with a structure for a performance which the local community and I do together. As you pointed out, the group work comes together quickly and spontaneously. And it's not like some kind of political organization is formed after the pulling and raising or toppling. That said, I am still in touch with many of the people I met in Standing Rock and Indonesia through Facebook and Instagram.
　Going back to 2008, when I took part in your project in Indonesia, soon after I came back to Japan and began my career as an artist, the 2011 earthquake hit. At the time, the work I was doing was basically a continuation of my graduation thesis at Musashino Art University. I was tracing the layout of my apartment and other private, personal spaces, recreating them as structures in public space, then having my friends help pull them with ropes to topple them or destroy them, in the style of what became "pull and topple." But the 2011

いるなかで、人が集まって家をモチーフにしたものを壊すことに疑問を覚えるのは当然でした。

　ちょうど震災翌日の3月12日に大阪城の目の前で「引き倒し」をする予定だったのですが、やはりその日のパフォーマンスは中止して、一昼夜この「引き倒し」をどうすればよいか考えました。その結果、従来のように構造体の自重に任せて一方向から勢いよく引っ張り倒すのではなく、あらかじめ横倒しにされた構造体を二方向からロープでゆっくり、音を立てないように引き起こすというプランに変更して、明くる日の3月13日に初めての「引き興し」（**H.H.H.A.（ホーム, ホテルズ, 秀吉, アウェイ）02**》）を行ないました。

　あくまでそれは即興的な措置だったので、震災後における「引き興し」のあり方についてきちんと考えるためにも震災後すぐ、福島県いわき市の豊間地区にボランティア活動をしに通い始めました。被災地で第一に復旧すべきライフラインが時間が経つにつれ徐々に安定してくると、今度は津波で壊された大量の家屋の瓦礫撤去が課題になりました。地元の土建屋さんが撤去するには量があまりにも膨大なんですよね。僕たちはそうした撤去作業のお手伝いをさせてもらいながら、瓦礫となったその材木を譲り受けていきました。各家の撤去作業の最終日、自分の家が全部片づけられる最後の瞬間には家主さんが避難所から見に来られるんです。撤去の現場で手伝っていると家主さんたちと話す機会が生まれ、この木を作品に使わせてもらえませんかってお願いしながら、少しずつ集めていきました。それを材料に塩屋埼灯台という地元のシンボルを復元し（津波で土台がダメージを受け消灯してしまっていました）、それを地域の人たちと一緒に引き起こしたのが《**The Lighthouses - 11.3 PROJECT**》です。文化の日である11月3日に、3月11日を逆にするというコンセプトで。そのときちょうど日本に帰国されていた関野さんにも参加いただいたんですが、どうでしたか？

関野：翼くんの作品は知っていて、ここで「引き倒し」はさすがにまずいんじゃないかって心配していたんだけど、行ってみたら灯台の「引き興し」だったので、こ

disasters made me rethink that. With hundreds of thousands of people losing their homes to the tsunami and having nowhere to live, or being forced from their homes by the meltdowns, I couldn't but question what I had been doing, which was essentially bringing people together to destroy structures in the shape of people's homes.

H.H.H.A. 02 2011

Actually, I had planned on conducting a "pull and topple" performance inside Osaka Castle Park on March 12. Then the earthquake and tsunami struck. I called off the performance and took a day to think about what to do about the whole "pull and topple" thing. I decided that, instead of pulling on a structure from a single direction and relying on the structure's weight for it to fall over, I would have people pulling on it from two different sides in order to raise it up, and slowly so as not to make any sound. That was my first "pull and raise" performance, a day later on March 13th, titled *H.H.H.A. (Home, Hotels, Hideyoshi, Away) 02.*

That method was only meant to be a stopgap solution. For various reasons, but also to think through the idea of "pull and raise," I started traveling to Toyoma in Iwaki, in southern Fukushima, soon after the disaster to help out as a volunteer. Once survivors and refugees were more or less settled, attention turned to the massive amounts of debris from homes destroyed by the tsunami. The amount was way beyond what local construction companies could handle. One of our tasks while helping to clear the debris was removing junk lumber from destroyed houses. On the last day when the clearing for a house was to be completed, the former owners would come from the refugee camps to watch. We talked to them, asked if we could use some of the lumber for an art project, and eventually collected enough to build a model of Shiozaki Lighthouse, a famous landmark in Iwaki that was knocked out of commission when the tsunami damaged its foundation. *The Lighthouses –11.3 PROJECT* was me and a mix of locals and refugees in Iwaki pulling and raising that structure together. The performance was held on Culture Day, November 3rd— in other words, on 11.3, the inverse of 3.11, March 11th, the day of the tsunami. Professor Sekino, you also participated. I think you had just returned to Japan.

Sekino: Yes. I had been following your work, and was honestly concerned about you doing a "pull and topple" performance in that context. But I was really pleased when I got there and saw you doing a "pull and raise" with the lighthouse instead. I was also surprised by how many people participated, so many more than in your graduation work.

れはいいなって思いました。参加人数も卒業制作とは全然違っていて驚いたね。

翼：卒業制作で初めて作った「引き倒し」作品《**g.g.g. 01**》は20人程度だったんですけど、いわきでは500人ほどの参加者だったので規模もまったく違いましたね。と同時に、津波という天災、原発事故という人災がコミュニティに対して与えたインパクトの大きさを実感しました。人類が自然と関わり合って生きていくなかでは天災とも向き合わなければならない局面が世界にたくさんあると思うんですが、関野さんが訪れた先で何か印象的な事例はありますか？

関野：僕が初めてペルーに行った1971年は、アンデスの山々の氷河の形が変わるくらい大きなアンカシュ地震に見舞われてからまだ1年後だった。アンカシュ州の州都ワラスでは建物の9割が崩壊して3万人もが犠牲となり、辺りはまだ瓦礫の山だったけれど、地元民同士で少しずつ助け合って震災から回復していく最中でもあって、その結束力の強さを感じたね。コミュニティの結束力というのは、都市よりも田舎のほうが強いだろうし、同じ都市でもより小さな町や地域ごとのほうが強い気がします。お互いに見知っていて、普段から助け合っている関係性。

翼：僕が《**H.H.H.H.**（ホーム, ホテルズ, ハルニャン, ハウス）》という作品で自分の実家を模した構造体を公共空間に放ったのは、埼玉県出身者として東京に中心性のなさを感じたからでもあります。個々人は都市の中で毎日無数の人々とすれ違いながらも一人の時間を確保していて、「プライベート」の価値がすごく高いですよね。そこに一石を投じる気持ちから、都市の真ん中に全然知らない人同士を結びつけてしまう媒介の働きをするひとつの対象を生み出したら、行き交う人々が互いを見る目が変わるんじゃないかと思ったんです。それとは逆に、震災時に掲げられた「絆」という言葉には、すでに関係性のある人同士なら言わなくても本質的に存在しているつながりを「あえて確認する」テーゼみたいな感触がありました。

H.H.H.H.（ホーム, ホテルズ, ハルニャン, ハウス）2008

事実として、「被災地」も人によって状況は多様です。運と言うと語弊があるか

Tsubasa: The first "pull and topple" work I did was my thesis project, *g.g.g. 01*, and I think about 20 people were involved. In Iwaki, it was like 500 people, so the scale was totally different. At the time, you could really feel the magnitude of the impact of the tsunami as a natural disaster and the meltdowns as a manmade disaster upon the local community. I realize that there are many examples across the world of people having to negotiate disasters as part of coexisting with nature. Are there any in particular that come to mind related to your travels?

Sekino: When I first went to Peru in 1971, it was only a year after the Ancash earthquake, which was strong enough to change the shape of glaciers in the Andes. In Huaraz, the capital of the Ancash region, some 30,000 people were killed and 90% of the buildings were destroyed. When I visited, the city was still filled with piles of rubble and locals were helping one another get back on their feet little by little. The solidarity was truly something to behold. I would hazard to guess that community solidarity is generally stronger in the countryside than it is in cities, and that even within a single city it's going to be stronger in smaller neighborhoods and districts, simply because people know each other and are used to helping one another on a regular basis.

Tsubasa: For *H.H.H.H.*, when I decided to create a model of my family home and put it in a public space, part of the reason was that, as someone from Saitama, Tokyo has no particular centripetal pull to me. People in cities pass by countless strangers on a daily basis, so they put a premium on "the private" and securing time for themselves. So, I wondered if maybe you could throw a wrench into that norm and change the way urban passersby look at one another by putting something into motion, smack in the middle of a city, which serves to bring strangers together. That whole discourse about "kizuna" ("bonds") that circulated after the earthquake and tsunami was the opposite of that, in the sense that it asked people to revisit connections that were already supposed to exist between them at a fundamental, unspoken level.

Even in the so-called "disaster zones," people's situations varied widely. Whether you call it luck or something else, even among the people I met in Toyoma, one person might have lost their entire family, their house, their job, everything, while their next-door neighbor was fine simply because their house faced a concrete building. That nagging question, "Why me? Why did I have to lose everything?," never really goes away. I heard many personal stories about how chance and luck decided life and death. Once you're there, you understand just how random and varied people's experiences were. So, the idea that a single word like "kizuna" could speak for everyone, and that anyone who doesn't fit that mold is excluded and made invisible, really felt like a form of violence to me.

Sekino: Soon after the tsunami, I went to Rikuzentakata in Iwate prefecture and helped deliver emergency supplies to people. Some of them weren't able to go to

もしれないけれど、僕が豊間地区で出会った人の中に家族全員、家も仕事も何もかも失くしてしまった方がいて、その隣の家はたまたま目の前にコンクリートのビルがあったおかげで無事だったので、「なぜ私がすべて失わなければならないのか？」という思いがずっと消えない様子でした。そのような偶然や運が生死を左右するケースが現地にはいくつもありました。それぞれの現況がバラバラなのはそこにいればわかるわけで、それを「絆」というひとつの言葉でまとめてしまうと、そこに属せない人を排除して見えなくさせる暴力性があるんと思うんですよね。

関野：僕も震災直後に岩手県の陸前高田市に行って、家が半壊で避難できなかったり家に老人や病人がいたりして避難所に入れない人たちに支援物資を持っていったことがあったんだけど、周囲に同調できなくて固まって過ごしていた。そういう弾かれた者同士のほうが避難所にいる人たちよりも結束力が強いように思った。

翼：「結束する」ってことは、自ずとそこに入れない者を生み出すことと同時ですよね。そして、集団から弾かれた人たちは移動を迫られる。結果、外部と内部という隔たりの関係が持続する。マレーシアのサバ州で2015年に行なった《**Break it Before it's Broken**》は、フィリピンのミンダナオ紛争から避難してきた難民の2〜3世代目にあたる無国籍者のコミュニティで制作した「引き倒し・引き興し」の作品ですが、彼女／彼らは大きな工場と工場とのあいだに自分たちでバラックのような家を建てて生活していました。僕が訪れたときにはすでに国の経済開発によって強制退去が決まっていて、そのコミュニティのリーダーに「政府がここを壊す前に僕たちで何かを壊してみませんか？」って提案したんです。なるべく彼らの家に近いものを作って、彼らと一緒にそれを壊したかった。

the shelters because their homes were only half-destroyed, or because they had family members who were elderly and sick and wouldn't be allowed to stay in the evacuation centers. Because their situations were exceptional, those people gravitated toward one another and survived by helping each other out. I got the sense that their solidarity, the solidarity among the outcast, was much stronger than that among people inside the evacuation centers.

Tsubasa: "Solidarity" creates not just an "us," but also a "them." And typically, the outcasts are pressured to move elsewhere, which reaffirms the gap between inside and outside. A project I did in Sabah, a state in Malaysia, in 2015, *Break it Before it's Broken*, was a "pull and raise/topple" project involving second- and third-generation, stateless refugees from the insurgency in Mindanao, in the Philippines. They lived in shanties they built themselves between the factory buildings where they worked. When I visited, the Malaysian government had already issued orders that the settlement be removed, in line with national economic development policies. I proposed to one of the community leaders, "Before the government comes and tears everything down, how about we destroy something ourselves?" So, we built a structure as close as possible to where they lived and destroyed it together.

No More "Frontiers" for Migrants
Tsubasa: Their homes were super rudimentary, just corrugated metal and lumber with raised floors. The structures for my performances are likewise made of simple materials, the reason being that I have to build the parts in one place, transport them to the performance site, and usually have access to the site for only a week or so. That's why, I try to make the parts as portable as possible. Since the refugees in Sabah are repeatedly forced to move, their homes are designed in a similar way, so they can pick up and leave at any time. I wanted to make a structure similar to their homes, and they wanted new materials for their next home, so I traded them: corrugated sheets and lumber I bought at the store for building materials used in their old homes. Sure enough, a few days after the performance, the authorities came to tear everything down, and they left in search of a new place to go. In terms of immigration problems, their case is extreme. Without anywhere to settle long-term, they have to constantly keep moving from place to place inside Malaysia. The government is also really underhanded. Because they want the "immigrant vote," the government hands out temporary residential permits, but they're only temporary. And since the refugees don't have citizenship, their children can't go to school. A local church pastor took it upon himself to teach them math. The curator I traveled with introduced me to the pastor, and it was because of him and our mutual trust that I was able to enter the community. You were saying earlier that solidarity is strongest among the outcast. Do you think that's true everywhere?

Sekino: Yes. After all, what are the mass migrations of

（＊）フィリピン政府によるキリスト教徒のミンダナオ島への入植政策に対して島のイスラム系住民の一部が抵抗し、1970年頃から分離独立を求める武力闘争に発展。40年以上続く紛争で十数万人が死亡し200万人以上が避難した。

もはや移民にとって「フロンティア」はない

翼：そもそも彼らの家はトタンや木材を使った高床式の、ものすごく簡素なつくりでした。僕が「引き倒し・引き興し」で作ってきた構築物の素材もとても簡易的なものなんですが、それはパフォーマンスをする場所が借りられても1週間かそこらで、本番では別の場所で作ったパーツをそこで組み合わせて作るから。できるかぎり運びやすいかたちを考えているんです。幾度となく移動を強いられてきた彼らの住居の工法も同じで、常に引っ越しや運搬に備えている。僕は彼らの家みたいな構築物を作りたいし、彼らは次なる住居へ向けた新しい素材がほしいので、僕が商店で調達してきたトタンや木材を彼らの建材と交換しながら制作していきました。パフォーマンスの数日後、実際に強制退去は執行され、彼女／彼らは新たな場所を求めて出発しました。

　ここにも移民問題の一端があって、ずっとマレーシア中をぐるぐる移動している彼らには安住できる居場所がない。卑怯なやり方だなと思ったのが、選挙時には「移民」の票もほしい政府は彼らに一時居住者ビザを配るけれど、あくまで一時的なものなのでやがて居住期限は切れてしまう。国籍のない子供たちは学校にも行けない。その子供たちにボランティアで算数を教えていたのが地域の教会の牧師さんで、同行していたキュレーターを介してつながった彼との信頼関係があったからこそ、僕はそのコミュニティの中に入ることができました。先ほど関野さんは「弾かれた者は結束が強い」とおっしゃっていましたが、それはどの世界でもそうなんでしょうか？

関野：そもそも人類の大移動そのものが弾かれた者の「グレートジャーニー」だからね。もちろん説はさまざまだけれど、人類がアフリカのサバンナを出たのは他の強い類人猿に押し出されたからという話があって、そこから自らの好奇心と向上心に従った大移動が始まった。あの山を越えたら何があるんだろう？という好奇心と、

human history but "the great journeys" of the outcast? Of course, there are various theories as to why the first human migrated out from the African savannah, but one theory proposes that they were pushed out by other hominoids and then kept on moving propelled by their own curiosity and hopes for a better future. A curiosity that asks, "I wonder what's beyond that mountain?" And a hope that says, "If we go there, maybe there's food and our lives will be better." The combination of the two is what compelled humans to spread out over the earth. After all, of all the animals, humans are the only species that you find in every corner of this planet.

When I went to Patagonia to visit the Yamana tribe, it was to meet the humans whose curiosity and hope had carried them the furthest. Because of environmental issues, hunting was already no longer an option for them. The area is mountainous, so they can't farm. They somehow manage to subsist on sea lions, fish, and shellfish they catch in the ocean. Yet, to my eyes, they did not seem particularly sturdy as a people. Also, connecting the eastern tip of the Malaysian peninsula and the Indonesian archipelago used to be a landmass known as Sundaland. During the Ice Age, the sea level lowered, exposing a vast area of land. When temperatures went back up, it was covered in water again, creating the network of islands that are there now. In the meantime, however, the population increased, so someone had to leave—the "weak," defined economically, politically, or socially. Pioneers who are able to convert frontier land into stable settlements stay on and survive, while the weak are forced out or die.

Tsubasa: With the stateless refugees in Malaysia I worked with in *Break it Before it's Broken*, even the new land they were headed to was already partitioned off and there was a good chance they would be mistreated there too. True "frontiers" are rare today. They didn't have electricity, so that was the first time I had to build a structure using only hammers and nails. I thought it was going to be a lot of work, but then everyone who helped me turned out to have excellent carpentry skills,

あの山を越えれば食べ物もあって暮らしが良くなるんじゃないか？という向上心。このふたつが結びついて世界中に人類は広まった。同じ種でこれほど全世界にくまなく行き渡った動物は人類以外にはいないよ。

その好奇心と向上心の最果て、いちばん遠くに行き着いた人類に会いに僕はパタゴニアに行ったわけだけど、彼らヤマナ族はそのとき環境的にすでに狩猟ができなくなっていた。山がちで農耕もできないので、海に入ってアシカや魚や貝を獲ってなんとか食いつないでいて、僕の目には強い人にはとても見えなかった。他には、マレー半島の東端からインドシナ半島にかけてあったと言われるスンダランドという土地は、寒冷期には海面が低下して広大な陸地となるけれど、気温が上昇すると海に沈んで小さな島々になってしまい、増えた人口のうち誰かが出ていかなくてはならない。弾き出されるのは経済的、政治的、あるいは社会的に「弱いやつ」。フロンティアではパイオニアとしてその土地を「住めば都」にした人間が生き残って、弱い者は移動を強いられるか、滅びてしまう。

翼：《**Break it Before it's Broken**》を一緒にやったマレーシア・サバ州の無国籍者たちだって、向かった先の新しい土地にはすでにテリトリーが張り巡らされていて、そこでもまた虐げられるかもしれない。現代ではもう「フロンティア」は見つけにくくなっていますよね。彼女／彼らのコミュニティには電気も通っておらず、そのとき初めてハンマーと釘だけで構築物を作ったんです。これは大変だなと思っていたら、協力してくれる皆が大工さんみたいな技術力を発揮して、あっという間に出来ちゃった（笑）。家を追われるごとに新たな家を作り続けている彼らは、聞けば普段から非正規の大工として働いたりしているらしいんです。でも、たとえば運悪く路上で職務質問されて警察に捕まると、彼らが「レッドハウス」と呼んでいた、いわゆる入国者管理収容所に入れられ、やがてフィリピンに移送されるものの彼らはフィリピン人でもないので政府も受け入れずにまたマレーシアに戻されて……というようにフィリピンとマレーシアをずっと行ったり来たりしているような状態でした。

それはまさに、そのとき同時に制作した作品《**I & see you**》の中で追いかけ／追いかけられる2人のようです。マレーシア国籍者と無国籍者の男性2人に街中で鬼ごっこをしてもらったのですが、国籍がなければ捕まって国外追放されることもあるけれど、国籍がないゆえに追放先の国にも入れない。でも、喧騒の街中を走り続けるかぎり、国籍がなければ書類の上では決して見つかりもしないんです。

経済が急成長中のマレーシアやインドネシアではいま、他の国や多国籍企業が工場を作るからというのが強制退去の口実になっています。経済成長と移民の問題はずっと密接に関わっていますよね。

関野：インドネシアでも、資源開発のために工場を立てるからと追い出された農民たちとそれを支援するラッパーたちが大統領官邸の前に座り込んで抗議活動をしていたね。官邸前ではテントを立ててはいけないらしく、それじゃあと彼らはテントを手で持って宙に浮かせていたよ（笑）。テント片手に訴えを全部歌詞に乗せて抗議を続けていたら、とうとう大統領と面会できることになって事態は変わったんだ。

so we finished in no time! A lot of them worked illegally as carpenters, since their houses are constantly being torn down and rebuilt elsewhere. If they're unlucky and get stopped on the street by the police and get interrogated about their employment status, they get sent to what they call the "red house," the immigration detention facility. Then, some of them might get deported to the Philippines, but they're not citizens there either, so the Philippine authorities reject them and they end up back in Malaysia, stuck in this pattern of being sent back and forth between the two countries.

I took up that topic in *I & see you*, which I made at the same time as **Break it Before it's Broken**. In the video, two men, a Malaysian national and a stateless refugee, are chasing each other in the city streets,

I & see you 2015

翼：そこでラッパーが介入してくるのが面白いですよね。僕も 2017 年にベトナムで、地元のアーティストたちと一緒にゲリラパフォーマンスの《**Guerrilla Waves**》をやったことがあります。ベトナムの刑法と政令は、公共空間で 5 人以上の市民が集会をする場合に人民委員会への事前申請を義務づけていて、却下ならまだしも内容によっては無視して許可を出さないことが日常的にあるようなんです。なので、公の場での集会そのものの僕の過去作品を見た同世代のベトナム人アーティストから「こんなことができるなんてうらやましい」と言われていて、何か持ち運び可能な物を使ってゲリラ的に行なうことを考えました。ベトナムの古都・フエの旧王宮前の広場に、監視員たちの昼休みを狙ってボートを 1 隻持ち込んで、ロープで引っ張り上げて倒して足早に立ち去ったんですが、もちろんボートは「移動」の道具のひとつであり、特にベトナム戦争の末期、国外逃亡の象徴でもありました。

Guerrilla Waves 2017

　ベトナムの若いアーティストたちがこれをアートとして肯定的に捉えてくれるかどうか、おそらく 20 年ほど前ならわからなかったんですが、今や彼らも海外に出ていったりネットを通じて海外の情報を得たりしているので、自ら疑問を抱いて行動する変化が起きているなと感じました。

関野：ベトナムでは人が自由に集まったりはできないのかな？

翼：体操とかはみんな自由にやっていますが、僕と一緒に滞在していたカンボジア人のアーティストは、ベトナム共産党の記念碑や政府施設の前で作品の写真撮影をして警察に捕まってましたね。おそらく条件は多々あって単に集まるだけでは捕まらないとは思うんですが、外国人が関わっていて、アートといった表現になると厳しく規制されるんだと思います。手伝ってくれたベトナム人のアーティストも何度も捕まっていて、警察との応酬に慣れてましたけど（笑）。

関野：かつて僕の知り合いのジャーナリストと作家が中国と北朝鮮とロシアの三国

playing tag. If you don't have citizenship and you're caught, they run you out of the country even though there's nowhere for you to go, precisely because you don't have citizenship anywhere. At the same time, since you don't exist on paper, as long as you keep running and hiding in the noise of the city, no one can track you.

With the economy growing so rapidly in Malaysia and Indonesia, and with other countries and multinational corporations building factories there, the authorities are using that as an excuse to evict people. Economic growth and immigration issues always seem to be go hand in hand.

Sekino: In Indonesia, I remember there were farmers displaced by the construction of plants for the processing of natural resources. They and a group of rappers who supported them staged a sit-in in front of the presidential palace. When they were told they couldn't set up tents there, they picked up the tents and held them in the air! Then they continued their protest, tents in one hand, rapping their complaints as lyrics, until finally the president agreed to meet with them. Their situation improved after that.

Tsubasa: I like the idea of having rappers be your voice. I did this secret performance with local artists in Vietnam called *Guerrilla Waves* in 2017. According to Vietnamese law and government ordinances, you have to have permission from the People's Committee for any congregation of more than five people in a public space. But not only do those requests regularly get rejected, you're lucky if they even bother to look at the reason. When Vietnamese artists my age saw my past work, they said they were really jealous about how I was able to stage them in public spaces. So, we decided to make something portable and do a guerilla performance with it in the square in front of the Imperial City in the ancient capital of Hue. We waited until the guards went on break, carried a boat to the square, used ropes to lift it up and topple it, then got out of there as fast as we could. A boat, of course, is a vehicle used for transportation. But in Vietnam, it is also a symbol of the refugees who were forced to flee their country toward the end of the Vietnam War.

Whether or not young Vietnamese artists would have accepted my performance as art twenty years ago, I'm not sure. But now, because a lot of them travel and they have access to information from abroad through the internet, I think they are starting to question their own situation more and find ways to transgress it.

Sekino: Is it really not possible for people to assemble freely there?

Tsubasa: Everyone does calisthenics and whatnot outdoors. But, for example, a Cambodian artist who was staying with me in Vietnam was detained by the police for taking photographs of her own work in front of government buildings and monuments to the Communist Party of Vietnam. I think it depends. I don't think people get arrested just for standing around. But once you have foreigners involved and you call it "art," they get stricter. The Vietnamese artists who helped me

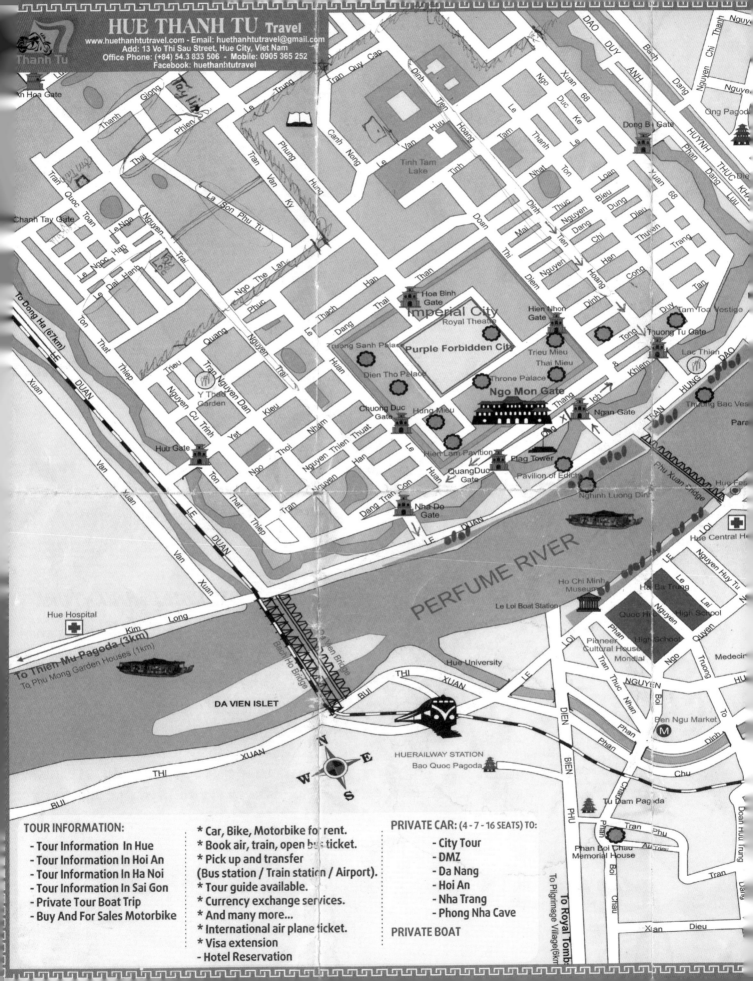

HUE THANH TU Travel

www.huethanhtutravel.com - Email: huethanhtutravel@gmail.com
Add: 13 Vo Thi Sau Street, Hue City, Viet Nam
Office Phone: (+84) 54.3 833 506 - Mobile: 0905 365 252
Facebook: huethanhtutravel

Thanh Tu

Imperial City
Royal Theatre
Purple Forbidden City
Truong Sanh Palace
Dien Tho Palace
Trieu Mieu
Thai Mieu
Throne Palace
Ngo Mon Gate
Chuong Duc Gate
Hung Mieu
Hien Lam Pavilion
Quang Duc Gate
Flag Tower
Pavilion of Edicts
Nha Do Gate
Nghinh Luong Dinh

Hoa Binh Gate
Hien Nhon Gate
Thuong Tu Gate
Tam Toa Vestige
Lac Thien
Thuong Bac Ves
Para
Ngan Gate

Dong Ba Gate
Ong Pagoda

Y Thao Garden
Tran Nguyen Dan
Hue Hospital

To Dong Ha (67km)
To Thien Mu Pagoda (3km)
To Phu Mong Garden Houses (1km)

DA VIEN ISLET

PERFUME RIVER

Ho Chi Minh Museum
Le Loi Boat Station
Hue University

Hue Central H
Hue Fes
Phu Xuan Bridge

Bach Ho Bridge
Da Vien Bridge

HUE RAILWAY STATION
Bao Quoc Pagoda

Quoc H High School
Pioneer Cultural House
Mondial
Ben Ngu Market
Medecin

Tu Dam Pagoda
Phan Boi Chau Memorial House

To Royal Tomb
To Pilgrimage Village (5km)

TOUR INFORMATION:

- Tour Information In Hue
- Tour Information In Hoi An
- Tour Information In Ha Noi
- Tour Information In Sai Gon
- Private Tour Boat Trip
- Buy And For Sales Motorbike

* Car, Bike, Motorbike for rent.
* Book air, train, open bus ticket.
* Pick up and transfer
(Bus station / Train station / Airport).
* Tour guide available.
* Currency exchange services.
* And many more...
* International air plane ticket.
* Visa extension
- Hotel Reservation

PRIVATE CAR: (4 - 7 - 16 SEATS) TO:

- City Tour
- DMZ
- Da Nang
- Hoi An
- Nha Trang
- Phong Nha Cave

PRIVATE BOAT

国境地帯に取材に行って捕まったんだけど、面白いのは尋問で最初に職業を聞かれるわけ。「ノベリスト」って答えたほうは「嘘を書くやつはいいよ」って寛大に扱われたんだけど、「ジャーナリスト」のほうはねちねちと尋問された。隠しておきたいことが暴露されちゃうからね。そこで「アーティスト」と答えたらどうなっていたんだろう？

翼：当局からすればジャーナリストが一番の標的だと思うんですが、情報を伝えるにしても、アーティストが作品を通して扱う時間のスパンって報道よりももう少し長いと思うんです。体制側としては隠蔽したい事実が作品の中に保存されて、下手したら20年、30年と海外の美術館で展示されてしまうかもしれない。そういう別視点での情報の保存・伝達能力がアートにはあると思うし、僕はそれがアートならではの力のひとつだとも考えているんですけど。

私たちが「ともに引っ張る」理由

翼：昨年の2020年にコロナ禍の香港で制作した《**Superstring Secrets: Hong Kong**》は、街中で集めた市民の秘密を一度全部シュレッダーにかけて、それをもとに巨大なロープを作る作品です。当局から常に監視され削除される民主化デモの情報をトレースするように。最終的にはデモに参加していたアーティスト、哲学者、学生との5人で、香港の地下通路上でロープを編む様子を撮影したんですが、彼女／彼らにとってその行為は反体制的表現のひとつとしてリスクでしかないんですよね。ベトナムやマレーシアでもそうですが、それを承知のうえで参加してくれるのはとてもありがたいと思いつつ、どうしてここまでやってくれるんだろうという疑問はいつも僕の頭をよぎります。

関野：「危ないのにどうして手伝ってくれるの」って聞いたりはしなかったんだね？そもそも、アーティストもプロテスターであるべきなのかな。

翼：マレーシアでは、「自分にはわからないけど、おまえにとっては大事なことなんだろ？」と言って手伝ってくれました。ベトナムではアーティストたちに「こういうことを自分たちもやっていかなきゃいけないんだ」っていう使命感があったからで、香港だとなにより彼女／彼ら自身がプロテスターだからですよね。作品として日本に持ち帰って展示して、香港の現状を日本の人たちに伝えてほしい、という思いも含まれていると思います。僕は自分をプロテスターだとは思わないですが、どんな言動にしろ抵抗の身振りにはリアリティがあります。外部者としての僕なりの視点と当事者としての彼女／彼らの視点をうまく合致させながら、そのリアリティを一時的で政治的なだけのパフォーマンスにではなく、「秘密」を通して公共と個人との関係性を問いかける普遍的な作品に仕上げたいと思ったんです。そのためにも、激しい攻撃にさらされ逮捕されてもずっと路上に出続ける、香港のそのダイナミズムの核にある人々の動機を知りたかった。

were all very used to being detained and dealing with the police!

Superstring Secrets: Hong Kong - Hang Hau 2020

Superstring Secrets: Hong Kong 2020

Sekino: Two friends of mine, a journalist and a novelist, got arrested while doing research near the border between China, North Korea, and Russia. The funny thing is that when they arrested them, the first thing the police asked them was, "What is your job?" The novelist replied, "I write fiction." "Oh, you write lies, that's fine," they said and let him go. But when my other friend said he was a journalist, they asked him tons of questions, because they don't want people like him exposing things they're trying to hide. I wonder what would happen if either of them had said, "I'm an artist."

Tsubasa: I imagine the authorities are most concerned about journalists. But if you think about how information circulates, I think artists generally deal with slightly longer spans of time than journalists typically do. An artwork might capture a reality that those in power want to hide, and if they're not careful, that could end up being shown in foreign museums for 20 or 30 years. Art is able to preserve and disseminate information in its own way. I think that's one of its strengths.

Why We Pull Together

Tsubasa: I was in Hong Kong when the pandemic hit in 2020. The work I made while there was *Superstring Secrets: Hong Kong*. I collected written secrets from people on the street, ran them through a paper shredder, and created a giant rope with the shreds. The project was meant to evoke the way in which the authorities had been surveilling and removing information pertaining to the pro-democracy protests. For the final performance, which I recorded on video, I had five people who had been involved in the protests–a philosopher, two artists, and two students–braid the rope together in one of the city's underground

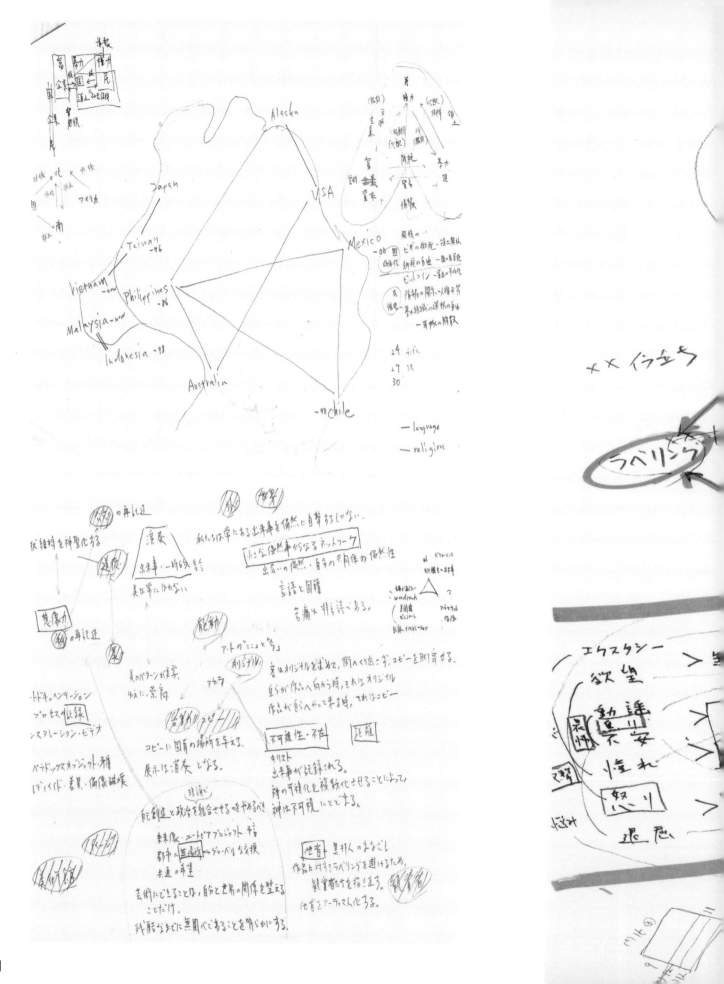

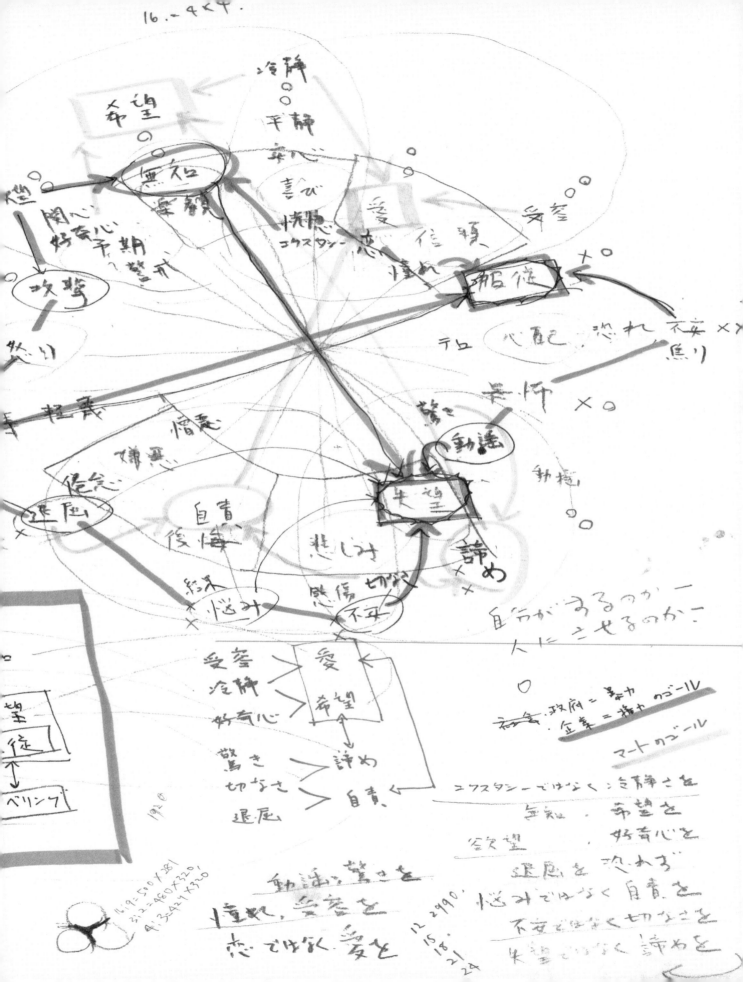

Superstring Secrets: Tokyo - Olympic Stadium 2020

Superstring Secrets: Tokyo - Tokyo Metropolitan Gymnasium 2020

tunnels. Being involved was a real risk for them, since the performance was essentially an act of protest against the government. Like in Vietnam and Malaysia, I was really thankful for people agreeing to participate despite them knowing the risks involved. But I also wonder what's in it for them.

Sekino: Do you ever ask them, "You know this is dangerous. Why are you helping?" But before that, a question for you: Do you think artists should be politically active?

Tsubasa: In Malaysia, people would say to me, "I don't know what your project is really about, but it's important to you, right?" So, they helped. In Vietnam, the young artists felt like it was their duty to be involved and do similar acts themselves. In Hong Kong, the participants themselves were already politically active. I suspect they also wanted me to exhibit the work in Japan so that Japanese would better understand the situation in Hong Kong. I don't think of myself as politically active, but I do believe that all words and actions of resistance, whatever their specific subject, have a certain weight and reality to them. While taking care that my perspective as an outsider matched up with theirs as insiders, my goal with *Superstring Secrets: Hong Kong* was not a political performance that momentarily engages the reality of the situation in Hong Kong, but rather something more universal, using the idea of "secrets" to question the relationship between the public and the individual. Behind the project was also a desire to understand what motivated people to continue protesting in the streets despite being repeatedly attacked and arrested, to understand what drove the people who were at the center of the dynamic movement in Hong Kong.

Sekino: Recently I was talking to Yusuke Kakuhata, an adventurer and writer, about how adventures are essentially "dis-systematic," about how they break with existing systems. "System" here can be understood in different ways. Traditionally, it refers to institutions or common sense. In that sense, adventurers are essentially "protestors." I personally think that the greatest adventure ever undertaken was when 82 revolutionaries, including Che Guevara and Fidel Castro, boarded the Granma in Mexico, a cheap yacht designed to carry only twelve people, and crossed the Caribbean Sea and landed in Cuba. What people like Magellan and Columbus did was impressive, of course. But their expeditions really only benefited Europeans. For the inhabitants of Africa and North and South America, who were colonized and almost wiped out by diseases brought over from Europe, it was a total disaster. I know opinion splits on what Guevara and Castro did afterwards, but it's hard to deny that they were heroes for ousting Fulgencio Batista and liberating the people of Cuba from his dictatorship. I think that art is also like an adventure. Makoto Aida's work, for example, I might describe as "dis-common sense." Inverting something and looking at it differently is one of the functions of contemporary art.

Superstring Secrets（無人島プロダクションでの展示風景）2020

関野：先日ちょうど角幡唯介という冒険家・作家と話していて、冒険は「脱システム」だという結論になった。ここで言う「システム」はいろんなものに置き換えることができて、昔であれば体制や常識。だから冒険する者は本質的にプロテスターなんだよね。僕自身は、革命家のチェ・ゲバラとカストロが12人乗りの安っぽいヨット（グランマ号）に82人で乗ってメキシコを出て、カリブ海を渡ってキューバに上陸する航海が最大の冒険だと思っています。もちろんマゼランやコロンブスもすごいけれど、彼らの冒険はヨーロッパ人に恩恵を与えただけで、アフリカや北米・南米の先住民にとっては植民地にされたうえに持ち込まれた病気で9割もの人間が死んでしまったりと、とんでもない。ゲバラとカストロのその後については評価が分かれるとは思うけれど、キューバの独裁者バティスタを倒して多くの人民を解放したそのときの彼らは正義だったと思う。僕はアートも冒険と似ていると思っていて、たとえば会田誠の表現は「脱常識」。物事をひっくり返して見方を変えるという現代アートの役割を果たしているよね。

翼：と同時にアートには記録的側面もあると僕は思っていて、保存され続ける作品自体は変わらずとも、時代が変わることによってその作品の見方が変わるということもあります。アート作品は新しい視点を開拓したり人の想像力を増幅したりしてこそ意味があると思っていて、その際に「体験」は切り離せないポイントです。それこそ僕の「引き倒し・引き興し」は現場の参加者も一緒に作品を体験しますよね。ただ、その一度きりの体験という要素が作品というコンテンツの最上位に来てしまうと、展覧会に訪れた人は作品の核を体験できない、ということだけが残ってしまう。だから僕は、パフォーマンスの体験から派生して展示される記録映像や物体や空間設計を通して、別の異なる体験を生み出すようにいつも挑戦しています。そういえば今回のコロナのパンデミックによって真っ先に減衰したのはそうしたフィジカルな体験や移動でしたが、これまで世界を自分の足を使って見てきた関野さんはこの状況をどう捉えていますか？

関野：人類史的なスパンで見ればこういうことは何回も起こっていて、結局は元に戻るんです。今回のコロナウイルスも1年じゃ無理だけど、4〜5年経てば収まるでしょう。ただ、ペストが流行したときと違って今回はグローバル化された現代社会を舞台にアマゾンの先住民にまで感染が広がってしまった。そういう観点で見ればもちろん今までの感染症とは歴史的に違います。

翼：そんなコロナ禍の下でも開催されそうな東京オリンピックと同時期に今回の僕の展覧会も開かれるんですが、香港でのプロジェクトを2020年の東京でも《**Superstring Secrets: Tokyo**》と題して行ないました。オリンピックの延期を受けて湾岸地帯の会場予定地がすべて工事中のまま閑散としていたのが象徴的だと感じ、そこを含めた都内各地にまたポストを置いて人々の秘密を集めました。他方、パンデミックで甚大な影響を受けた人たちをリサーチするなかで、「夜の街」で働いていたフィリピンパブの従業員とか、仕事がなくなってしまった外国人労働者のほかに、埼玉のクルド人のコミュニティで生活している方に出会いました。その方は1990年代から日本にいるんですが、在留ステータスがずっと「仮放免」なので

Tsubasa: I agree, but I think that art also has a documentary function. A finished, preserved work itself might not change over time, but the way people see and interpret it will. What makes art important, I think, is its ability to open up new perspectives and expand people's imagination. "Experience" is essential to that. With my "pull and raise" and "pull and topple" works, I experience the artwork together with everyone participating in the performance. However, if that one-time experience becomes the most important aspect, people who see the work in a gallery won't be able to share in that core experience. That's why one of the biggest challenges in my work is how to create an experience that is at once based on the original performance yet distinct from it through video documentation, displayed objects, and installation design. Speaking of physical experience and movement, the coronavirus pandemic has had a direct and immediate impact on reducing both. I wonder how that makes you feel, as someone who has crisscrossed the world, much of the time on foot.

Sekino: Pandemics have happened many times over the course of human history, and eventually things always return to normal. It's not going to be one year, but probably in four or five the coronavirus pandemic will be under control. But unlike, say, the plague in the past, this time the pandemic was global, reaching from advanced modern societies all the way to the indigenous peoples in the Amazon. In that sense, we are dealing with something new.

Tsubasa: Well…despite the pandemic, not only are the Olympics going ahead as planned, so is my exhibition. After I returned to Japan in May 2020, I did a version of my Hong Kong project titled *Superstring Secrets: Tokyo*. With the Olympics postponed, construction on the various sporting facilities around Tokyo Bay was suspended. Walking around, I was struck by what a ghost town the whole area had become, so I decided to put a postbox there and at other places in Tokyo to collect people's secrets, like I had in Hong Kong. In the process of trying to get a sense of how badly people

入管の収容施設に何度も入って、中でハンガー・ストライキをしたこともあるそうです。何度も難民申請をして裁判も起こしたんですが負けてしまった、と。僕も知らなかったんですが、「仮放免」は申請をして許可を得ないかぎり県境を越えてはいけないらしく、感染拡大時の「越県しないで」というアナウンスをよそに彼が、「そもそも僕たちはずっと越県が許されてなくて（他県にいる）家族とも自由に会えないんだよ」と言っていたのが胸に突き刺さりました。

彼の周りのクルド人コミュニティには解体業の従事者が結構いて、一時はオリンピック需要で仕事が増えていたのが延期になって現場が止まり、皮肉なことに、建設現場の人手不足を補っていた彼らから先に切られていました。オリンピックと移民の問題がパンデミックを通じて顕在化していると感じた僕は、秘密が書かれシュレッドされた紙で大きなロープを編むパフォーマンスを陸上競技場で撮影させてもらえないかと、彼女／彼らにお願いしたんです。

移民・難民をテーマにした作品といえば、2016 年にアメリカ・オレゴン州のポートランドで制作した《**The Raft of** _____》もそうですね。プラスチックの樽と木製パレット、2 人用テントを組み合わせて作った即席の筏（いかだ）でウィラメット川を出発し、自力で漕げるところまで漕いで、力尽きた地点で QR コードを掲げます。美術館でその QR コードを読み込むと、Google マップ上にその筏の位置情報、つまり鑑賞者へ向けられた SOS 信号が出てくるんですけど、実はフェイクの情報なんですよね。位置情報はあたかも漂流が続いているかのように毎日ウェブ上を移動しているんですが、実際は全然移動してないんです。つまり救うべき僕らはいまそこにはいないけれど、逆にそこには本当に遭難している人がいるかもしれない。

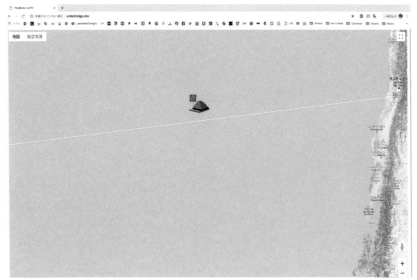

The Raft of _____ 2016

この作品はシリアからたくさんの難民が出た 2016 年に、アメリカ滞在中に制作しました。緊迫するシリアの難民問題はパリをはじめ西欧諸都市で同時多発したテロとも結びついていて、紛争介入したアメリカにも関わっているわけですが、当時真っ只中だった大統領選挙ではそのことが大きな争点にならずに、経済政策や税制、保険制度や銃規制、アメリカへの移民・難民に対する処置といったアメリカの内政

had been impacted by the pandemic, I met someone who worked at a Filipino bar in a quasi-red light district, a foreign laborer who was out of work, and a member of the Kurdish community in Saitama. The Kurdish guy had been living in Japan since the '90s, but as he was only given "provisional" residential status, he has ended up in the Immigration Bureau's detention center in Shinagawa multiple times, and even staged a hunger strike there. He has applied for refugee status repeatedly, and has even gone to court, but lost. I didn't know this, but if your residential status is only provisional, you can't leave the prefecture you live in without permission from Immigration. So, when the pandemic got bad and the government told everyone not to cross prefectural lines, all he could say was, "We're not allowed to go to other prefectures anyway, not even to see our families!" It was heartbreaking to hear that.

The Raft of _____ 2016

A lot of the Kurds in his community work in demolition. Initially, they had a lot of work because of the Olympics, but when the games were postponed their work was also halted. Immigrants had been brought in to fill the labor shortage at construction sites, but of course they were also the first people cut when things got tight. I think the pandemic really brought into focus certain contradictions between the Olympics and immigrants in Japan. So, I asked people from the Kurdish community if they might let me shoot them braiding a rope made of shredded secrets, this time at a track and field stadium.

The Raft of _____ was another work I did about immigrants and refugees, back in 2016 in Portland, Oregon. I made an impromptu raft out of wood pallets and plastic barrels, with a two-person tent on top, and

の話に終始していたんですよね。知らないわけはないのに争点化されない情報と、今いる場所からは見えない悲惨な現実とのずれ。情報という海の上でその真実と虚偽とのあわいを「漂流」するような作品になりました。

関野：たしかに実際の漂流と違ってこのフェイクの漂流で人が死ぬことはないよね。でも、「争点にならない」という事態はいろんなところで起きている。たとえば、永世非武装中立を宣言しているコスタリカには軍隊はいないんだけど、1986年に就任したオスカル・アリアス・サンチェス大統領がアメリカのニカラグア政策に不支持を表明したり、グアテマラで国際会議を開いて中米和平に貢献したりしてノーベル平和賞まで受賞するくらい大活躍したんだけど、再任のために憲法改正を図るも失敗した。結局、国民にとって外交は争点にならない。遠くの紛争よりもここでの毎日の生活のほうが大事なんだよね。

翼：そういう意味でいうと、福島でもマレーシアでもスタンディングロックでも、僕の「引き倒し・引き興し」の共同作業に参加してくれた人たちは、本当は明日どうやって食べていくかがいちばん大事なのに、それとは一見無関係どころか無意味にも見えることに楽しそうに参加してくれました。僕たちがコミュニティや他者に対して持つ利他的な本能をそこに垣間見るのですが、人にはどこかしら損することを選ぶ能力がありますよね。

関野：共感能力があって共同して利他的な行動を取れるのが人間の特徴だよね。チンパンジーはコミュニティを作ったけれど家族は作らなかった。一方ゴリラは雄ゴリラが子と遊んだりして父親の兆しの行動を取る。家族の始まりと言っていいのだけど、母ゴリラが他の雌またはつがいと敵対関係にあって、コミュニティを作らなかった。「見返りを求めない家族の論理」と「見返りを求める、あるいは互いを平等に扱うコミュニティの論理」という相反するようなふたつの論理をうまく調整し

launched it out into the Willamette River. We paddled as far as we could go, until we got tired, then posted a QR code of our location. If you scanned that code in the museum, you could see on Google Maps where we were. It was like an SOS signal, with a new location uploaded every day as if we were floating adrift, but a fictional one, since we were actually in the river only for the first day. However, though *we* weren't at that location, maybe someone who is actually stranded and in need of help was.

I made this work while living in the United States, when the refugee crisis because of the Syrian Civil War was reaching its peak. As things got worse, there were terrorist attacks across Europe and the Western world, and then America and other foreign countries got involved in the war. During the 2016 US presidential election, however, they didn't really talk about Syria, focusing instead on economic policies, taxes, health insurance, gun rights, et cetera. When they talked about immigrants and refugees, it was only about the domestic situation in the US. They know something is a serious issue, yet don't talk about it. Real tragedies are happening, but they're invisible from where you're standing. Being "adrift" between falsehoods and truth in a sea of information was what **The Raft of _____** was essentially about.

Sekino: With a fictional boat at sea, no one is going to die, of course. But the fact you point to, about how important things don't get debated, happens in a lot of places. For example, Costa Rica has declared itself permanently neutral and doesn't have a military. After he became the country's president in 1986, Óscar Arias Sánchez declared that he refused to support US policies in Nicaragua and helped set up an international convention to broker peace in Central America, landing him a Nobel Peace Prize. Nonetheless, his popularity was still not great enough to overturn a constitutional ban against president's seeking re-election. Citizens of a country don't really care about foreign diplomacy. They care more about their everyday lives, here and now, than about wars far away.

て、類人猿でヒトだけが家族とコミュニティを同時に形成することに成功したんだ。

翼：「見返り」という観点で「引き倒し・引き興し」を考えてみると、ロープを引っ張って構造体を動かすという「労働」への見返りを参加者から求められたこともなければ、そもそも引っ張る体験をある種の「娯楽」として提供することに対する見返りを僕が参加者に求めたこともありません。一方で「こういう人でなければ参加できません」というような限定をしたこともなく、常に参加条件はオープンで平等であることも「引き倒し・引き興し」の特徴のひとつです。そうした状態をキープできるのは、「一人では動かせない物をグループでなんとか動かす」というゴールは具体的でありながらも、それを動かす、倒す、壊す、起こすことによって何が生まれるのかがどこまでも抽象的だからだと思います。この点が、僕たちがクジラを引っ張る動機と「引き倒し・引き興し」でロープを引っ張る動機との違いを生んでいるのかもしれません。

　マレーシアでのプロジェクトのように、政府に家を壊される前に自分たちで家を壊したところでその先に救いはないかもしれない。けれど「とりあえずやってみよう」と楽しげに参加してくれる姿を見ると、ただただ好奇心が人々を突き動かしているんだなと実感するんです。それは自分の力の限界を知ることで初めて芽生える他者への好奇心や、グループで共同作業することで初めて踏み出せる新たな行動範囲への好奇心に、どこかでつながっているのではないでしょうか。

（2021 年 6 月、都内にて対談を収録）

Tsubasa: If you applied that to my "pull and raise" and "pull and topple" works, I suppose you could say that, whether it's Fukushima or Malaysia or Standing Rock, what's most important to people is how they'll be able to feed themselves tomorrow, yet still they found enjoyment in participating in performances that, on the surface, are meaningless and have nothing to do with their daily lives. In that, I think we can glimpse a natural altruism within communities in their regard of outsiders, but also a human inclination to choose to do things that don't necessarily benefit them in a direct way.

Sekino: Acting collectively and altruistically really does seem like a defining quality of being human. Chimpanzees create communities, but not families. With gorillas, the males will play with their offspring and act outwardly like fathers, while mother gorillas are antagonistic toward other females and even their own mates. They create something like families, but not real communities. Among all the primates, only humans have managed to create both families and communities. They somehow put together two seemingly mutually opposed things: "families that don't expect anything in return from their members" and "communities in which everyone is treated equally and expects something in return from other members."

Tsubasa: Thinking about my "pull and raise" and "pull and topple" projects from the perspective of the kind of interpersonal "expectations" you're talking about, participants in my performances have never asked for anything in return for providing their "labor" to pull ropes and move the structures I build. Likewise, I have never expected anything from them for providing a sort of "entertainment" in the form of the experience of that activity. Also, I have never stipulated what kind of person is allowed to participate. Participation open to all people equally has always been a feature of my "pull and raise/topple" works. That has led to my performances having a concrete goal—moving something that is too big for an individual—while the something that is supposed to result from the activity of moving, toppling, destroying, raising, et cetera, stays abstract. I think this is where the motivation for pulling and raising in an artistic context is very different from, say, collectively pulling a whale ashore, like we witnessed in Indonesia.

　With my project in Malaysia, there might be something sad and desperate about having people destroy their homes themselves before the government comes and does so. But seeing how much the participants enjoyed doing so "just for the hell of it" really made me realize how powerful simple curiosity can be as a motivating factor for people. Somewhere, somehow, I feel like that's connected to the way in which people become curious about others once they realize the limits of their own strength, and how they become curious about new fields of action once they get involved in collective, group-based work.

(June 2021, Tokyo)

パラドックスと緊張の網
（悖論與張力之網）

ワン ウェイウェイ
王 慰 慰
Centre for Heritage, Arts and Textile（CHAT）キュレーター

The Net of Paradox and Tension

Wang Weiwei
Curator, Centre for Heritage, Arts and Textile (CHAT)

「あいちトリエンナーレ2019」での加藤翼の作品《2679》は私にとって強く印象に残った。映像の中では、日本の伝統音楽の演奏家が3名それぞれ離れた位置に立ち、紐で互いに結ばれ動きを制限された状態で日本の国歌「君が代」を演奏しようとしていた。結果として曲は断片的になり、判別できなくなる。この傑作の歴史的意義はそのタイトル、《2679》に隠されていた——1940年は日本の皇紀2600年に当たるとして、皇居前の広場には5万人ちかくの市民が集まり国歌を歌って祝った。同時に、オリンピックと万国博覧会が東京で開催されるはずだった1940年は日本のナショナリズムが高まった年としても知られている。興味深いことに、皇紀であれば2679年に当たる2019年のあいちトリエンナーレで展示された作品のいくつかは「従軍慰安婦問題」や「皇室」に対する批判的な表現があったため綿密にチェックされ、日本社会と世界のアートシーンは大きく揺れ動いた。この展覧会は一部の右翼によって強く批判され、いくつかの作品はしばらくのあいだ展示を中断させられるまでに至った。

In Aichi Triennale 2019, Tsubasa Kato's videography work *2679* left a great impression on me. In the video, three traditional music performers were tied to each other by a rope and tried to play the Japanese national anthem *Kimigayo* at a distance from each other, with their movements constrained by the rope. The anthem, as a result, is fragmented and incomprehensible. The historical significance of this masterpiece was hidden in its title *2679*: In 1940, in celebration of the 2,600-year legacy of the Imperial House of Japan, nearly 50,000 citizens gathered and sang the Japanese national anthem on the square before the Imperial Palace. Concurrently, 1940 was also regarded as the year of the rise of Japanese Nationalism as Japan was hosting both the Olympics and the World Expo that year. Interestingly enough, a number of the artworks showcased in Aichi Triennale 2019, held on the 2,679th anniversary of the Imperial House of Japan, were scrutinized due to their criticism of "Comfort Women Issue" and "the Imperial House of Japan", causing a commotion in the Japanese society and the international art scene. The exhibition was heavily criticized by some right-wing politicians, even the showing of some artworks had to be suspended for a while.

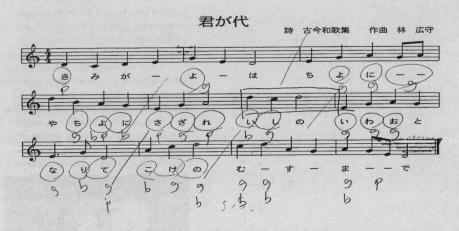

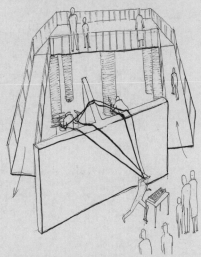

同じ年、香港では民主化デモのために百万人もの人々がストリートに出て、中国中央政府による「一国二制度」や香港の独立司法の破壊に対して抗議した。直接的なリーダーシップの統率なしにソーシャルメディアによって駆動されたこの社会運動は1年ちかく続き、もともとのデモ行進や座り込みから徐々に激化して、市民と警察との暴力的対峙や全面的な社会的分断を引き起こした。そしてこの運動が落ち着き始めたときに、中国の武漢で発生したとされる新型コロナウイルスがあっという間に世界的に猛威を振るったのである……。

コロナウイルスが香港で蔓延する少し前、加藤翼が大館當代美術館での展覧会に招待されていたのがきっかけで私たちはこの香港という文化的・政治的な激震地で

In the same year, the Anti-Extradition Law Movement brought millions of citizens to the streets of Hong Kong, protesting the undermining of the "One Country, Two Systems" and of Hong Kong's Judicial Independence by the Chinese Central Government. Without any unified direct leadership, this social media-driven social movement lasted for the greater part of the year, and

知り合い、私は彼の作品への理解を深めていった。香港に数か月滞在した加藤は《**Superstring Secrets: Hong Kong**》という作品を制作した。香港の街中にある歩行者用地下通路で撮影されたこの映像作品の中では、5人の若いアーティストと学生たちが社会運動でよく使われるようなヘルメットを被り、地面にしゃがみこみながら、細断された紙を束ねて太い「紙の縄」を2本撚り上げようとしている。これらの紙片は加藤が収集した秘密で――彼は投票箱のようなものをいくつか香港の地下通路に設置し、道行く人々に自身の「秘密」を紙に書いてもらった――その紙をシュレッダーにかけてバラバラにしたあとロープに束ねた。映像の中でパフォーマーのヘルメットは白く長い管によってつながれていて、行動範囲や動作が制限されながらもお互いに協力せざるをえない状況に置かれている。

　この作品は明らかに、加藤が香港の社会運動を観察して考えたことを表している。香港に来る前に加藤は台湾にも短期間滞在していて、その間そこからも香港の社会運動を注視していた。台湾の若い世代による香港の社会運動への支持と増幅する「反中国」の感情の中にいたことで加藤は、中国本土、香港、台湾の複雑に絡み合った関係をも直接的／間接的に体感することができた。台湾海峡の安全保障に関わっている日本と韓国、そして長らくアジアと深くつながっているアメリカも、この混沌とした海域を攪拌（かくはん）する重要な勢力である。

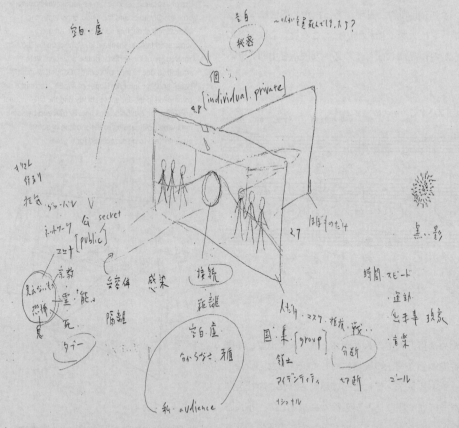

Superstring Secrets: Hong Kong 2020

escalated from initial parades, sit-ins, and chants to violent stand-offs between civilians and the police and a complete social rift. As the movement was starting to die down, an outbreak of the COVID-19, which was first confirmed to occur in Wu Han, China, swept the globe suddenly…

Shortly before the Coronavirus spread to Hong Kong, Tsubasa Kato was invited to attend an exhibition of Tai Kwun Contemporary, through which we became acquainted in this cultural and political epicenter, and I gained more understanding of his works. Kato created *Superstring Secrets: Hong Kong* after having stayed in Hong Kong for several months. In this video recording of a performance taken place in an underpass in Hong Kong, five young artists and students wearing protective helmets commonly used in the social movement, crouched down to the ground, and tried to roll two oversized strings made from lots of shredded paper. These shredded pieces of paper were originally notes of written secrets: Kato had placed several installations resembling voting booths in different underpasses in Hong Kong and invited people to write down their secrets on pieces of paper, before shredding and twisting them into superstrings. In the clip, the helmets the performers were wearing were connected to a long white tube, restraining actions and moving areas of the performers, forcing them to coordinate.

Needless to say, this piece reflects Kato's observation and thoughts about the social movements in Hong Kong. Before coming to Hong Kong, Kato also visited Taiwan for a short period, during which time he paid close attention to the social movement in Hong Kong

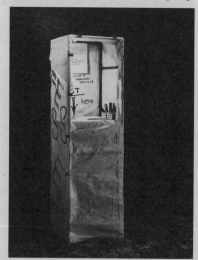

　加藤翼は近年、自身の参加型パフォーマンス作品においてしばしば、一見すると無茶で荒唐無稽なミッションや目標を設定し、人々に参加してもらうことで共同で作品を完成させている。たとえば、マレーシアのサバ州における難民のコミュニティでは、簡素な家屋から木材を集めて大きな家のような木造の構築物を制作し、

地域の人々とともにロープで引き倒して破壊した。また、ベトナムで現地のアーティストたちとともに行なったゲリラパフォーマンスでは、警備員が昼休憩に入るのを待ってからボートを旧王宮前の芝生の上まで運び、ひっくり返してから素早く立ち去った。そしてまた、朝鮮半島と日本列島とのあいだにある島（韓国語では「テマド」、日本語では「対馬」と呼ぶ）では、言語の壁によってほとんど意志の疎通もできない、出会ったばかりの韓国人男性と一緒に、加藤はQRコードが描かれたサインボードをボートで近くの無人島まで運び、協力してその島に打ち立てた……。一見突拍子もないこうした行動の背後にあるのは、それぞれのコミュニティにおける社会や文化に対する加藤の応答であり、近年のアジア遠征を通じて彼がアジア諸国間の複雑な関係についてどう考えたのか、その思考をそこに垣間見ることができる。

remotely. The support from young generations for the social movement and the heightened Anti-China sentiment in Taiwan, allowed him to directly and indirectly experience the intricate and intertwined relationships between Mainland China, Hong Kong, and Taiwan. The United States, who has been deeply involved in the security of Taiwan Strait for a long time, along with Japan and Korea, is also a crucial force impacting this sea in turmoil.

Break it Before it's Broken（スケッチ）2015

　マレーシア・サバ州での作品《**Break it Before it's Broken**》は、フィリピン・ミンダナオ地域でのモロ紛争によって居場所を失って流れてきた難民を追放するマレーシア政府に立ち向かう、一種の集団的「暴力」を通じたカーニバル調の抗議だった。木材でできた構築物を引き起こしては引き倒し、木の「家」が何度も地面に叩きつけられるたびに「構築」と「破壊」の境界はなくなっていく。ベトナムでゲリラ的に行なわれた《**Guerrilla Waves**》は、言論の自由が抑圧されがちなベトナム社会において市民を「無視」しようとする当局に対する遊び心のある挑発だった。そして、互いの言語を理解しない加藤と韓国人との共同作品《**言葉が通じない**》では、日本と韓国とのあいだで長年領土的な問題となっている対馬海峡が舞台になっている。この作品は鑑賞者にも参加を促し、展覧会でそのQRコードを読み取るとGoogleマップ上にはサインボードが立てられた島が現れるが、ウェブ上に表示されるのは実際には緯度と経度の単なる数値にすぎない。そうする

Throughout Kato's series of participatory performance videos in recent years, he often set a seemingly absurd goal or mission, and invited others to participate and finish the artwork together. For instance, in a refugee community in Sabah, Malaysia, he once collected lumber from crude houses and assembled it into a large house-like wooden structure, then invited people from the community to tear down the structure with a rope. He has also collaborated with a group of local Vietnamese artists on a guerrilla performance on the open lawn in front of the former palace—they waited for moments when the guards went on lunch breaks, dragged a boat to the lawn, toppled it and quickly left. Another time, on an island located between the Korean peninsula and the Japanese archipelago ("Daemado" in Korean; "Tsushima" in Japanese), Kato and a Korean guy he just met who could barely understand each other due to the language barrier, carried a signpost with QR cord to another deserted island nearby through kayaking, they took turns to carry the signpost and planted it on the island. Behind all these seemingly absurd acts were Kato's responses to the social cultures of different locations, through which we can catch a glimpse of his thoughts from his recent Asia expedition on the intricate relationship between Asian countries.

ことで加藤は、国民国家におけるテリトリーの問題を現実からバーチャル空間へと
シフトさせ、次のような質問を提起する――国際政治の場で常に論争の的になるこ
の島の帰属問題は、両国の人々にとってどのような意味があるのだろうか？　互い
の言語を理解できない人間同士が実際に対面するとき、彼らは想像力や直感を使っ
てどのように行動しコミュニケーションをとるのだろうか？　作品の中で韓国人の
男性はこう言っていた。「私はあなたが言っていることがわからないから、理解で
きない。だから、空気を読むんだ。シンプルに、その場の空気を感じて、その自然
な直感に従うんだ」。コミュニケーションの難しさを実際に引き起こしているのは、
理解を妨げる障壁ではなく、理解しようとする誠意なのだ。

　2019年以前の作品と比べると、2020年初頭の香港で制作された加藤翼の作品は
少し変化したように思える。パンデミックにより帰国を余儀なくされた加藤は東
京の個展で《**Superstring Secrets: Hong Kong**》を展示した（「**Superstring
Secrets**」、無人島プロダクション、2020年10月）。このとき、「紙の縄」は映像を飛び
出して展覧会場の床にまで伸びるように展示され、周りには細かな紙片がたくさん
散乱していた。映像には過去の作品と比べて「引っ張り」「衝突」「暴力」「破壊」

といった表現が少なく、そのような外に
向けたエネルギーの代わりに、制限され
た動作とぎこちなさが描写されていた。
映像中のパフォーマーたちは落ち着いて
規律的な動作でロープを捻じりながらも、
上からパラパラと落ちて床を散らかして
いく紙屑はどうすることもできず、無力
だった。しいていえば最大の「暴力」的
表現は天井から吊るされたシュレッダー
かもしれない――人々の秘密が書かれた
紙はベルトコンベアでシュレッダーまで
運ばれ、耳をつんざくような大きな音と
もに大量の紙片が天井からいきなり降り
注ぐ。その瞬間、取り組むべきミッショ
ンや実現可能なゴールがすべて消滅して
しまうようで、鑑賞者は不安や無力感、
そしてどうしようもない状況に置かれた

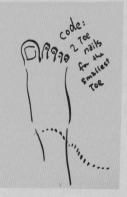

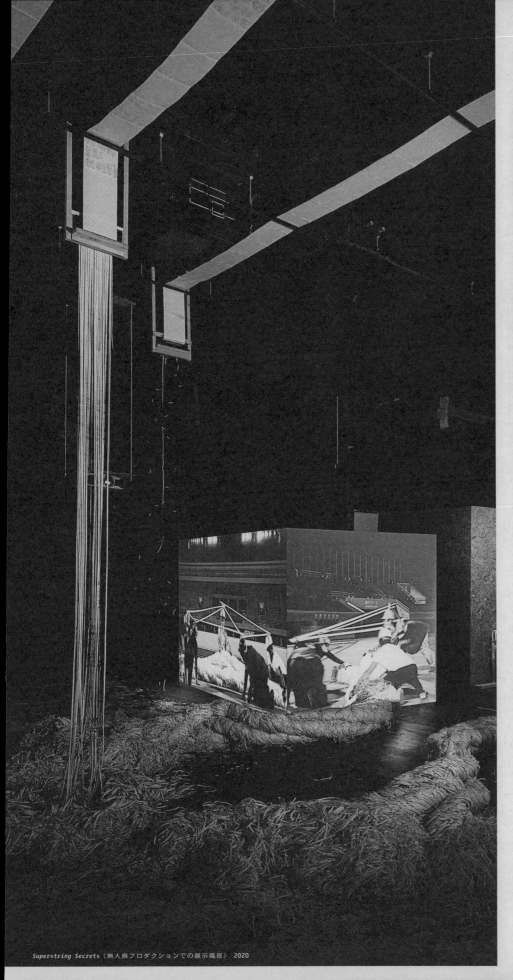

The work **Break it Before it's Broken** in Sabah, Malaysia
was a carnivalesque protest through collective "violence"
against the Malaysian Government, on its expulsion of
refugees displaced by the Moro conflict in the Mindanao
region of the Philippines–by pulling up and tearing
down the wooden structure, the boundary between
"construction" and "destruction" became blurred as the
wooden "house" was brought to the ground again and
again. **Guerrilla Waves**, the guerrilla performance that
took place in Vietnam, was a playful provocation
towards the negligence of citizens from the Vietnamese
authorities in a society where Freedom of Speech was
often oppressed. As for the artwork **They Do Not
Understand Each Other**, a collaboration between Kato
and the Korean who couldn't understand each other,
the background was set in the Tsushima Strait, an area
that had been under chronicle territorial dispute
between Japan and Korea. The artwork invites
participation from visitors, encouraging them to scan
the QR code that prompts the geographic coordinates
of the island where the signpost was planted, then to
find it on Google Map. By doing so, Kato shifted
territorial dispute between two modern nations from
reality to virtual space, which begs the question: what
does territorial dispute mean to the people of these two
nations when it is a constant topic in international
political affairs? In real life encounters where people are
not able to understand each other due to the language
barriers, how do they act and communicate with human

感覚に襲われる。つまりこの作品は、アジアの複雑な関係性に直面して未来への道を模索できないかと加藤とともに考える人々の、リアルな現実や感情を表現しているのだ。

　　世界で最も多様な地域のひとつだと言えるアジアは、一括りにして扱うのが困難な対象であり、それは地理的な空間だけでなく、政治的概念でありながらも文化的

instincts and imagination? As the Korean said in the video, "I don't understand, cause I don't know what you're saying. I just feel the atmosphere, just a simple feeling and then, naturally follow the atmosphere." The real cause of communication difficulties is not the obstacles themselves, but the willingness to communicate.

Compared with Kato's works prior to 2019, his works in Hong Kong in early 2020 seemed to have changed a little. Forced to return to Japan because of the pandemic, Kato showcased his artwork *Superstring Secrets: Hong Kong* in an exhibition in Tokyo (*Superstring Secrets*, MUJIN-TO Production, 2020). This time, the paper string shown in the video extended out to the exhibition floor, surrounded by more shredded paper. There was less hauling, clashing, destroying, and forcing through that was prevalent in Kato's previous works, as outward forces were held back and replaced by constrained actions in awkwardness. In the video, the performers were twisting the superstring in a calm and conforming manner, while feeling completely helpless as small pieces of the superstring kept falling out and making a mess on the floor. Perhaps the greatest source of "violence" was the paper shredder hanging from the ceiling: notes with people's secrets were transported to the shredder on a conveyor belt, then in the piercingly loud noise from shredding, loads of shredded paper were poured down from the ceiling without notice. In this moment, any directional mission or achievable goal seemed to vanish; rather, we were left with anxiety, hopelessness, and an unfixable mess. In other words, this piece of work reflected the reality and emotions of Kato and those who try to find a way out when facing the intricate relationships in Asia.

As one of the most diverse regions in the world, Asia is not a subject that can be treated as one single unit directly. It is not only a geographical concept, but also one of politics, culture, as well as certain measures of value. In this vast region where land and ocean converge, multiple civilizations have coexisted for a long time, mixed, and infiltrated each other, yet never assimilated or unified as one. Since the end of the 19th century, everywhere in Asia has experienced internalization of western values caused by colonization. The internalized western values have been transformed by different ethnic groups in Asia into their own ideological power and identification mechanism, which brings more differences, conflicts, and intertwined relationships on various levels. The most excruciating experience in modern Chinese history was entangled with Japan; In the Cold War landscape, the country's complicated relationships with Japan, the Korean Peninsula, and Taiwan were also inseparable from the confrontation with the United States. In recent years, the rapid rise of China, along with its political rivalry and competition in trade and technology with the United States, has repeatedly brought tension to the neighboring regions. The imbalance between heavy interdependence in the economy and the conflicts in politics and national security, the overlaps between

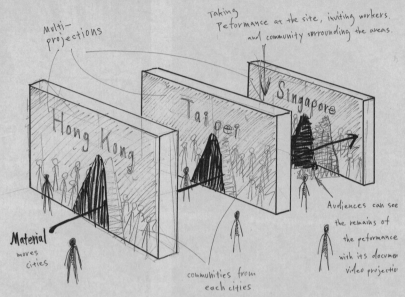

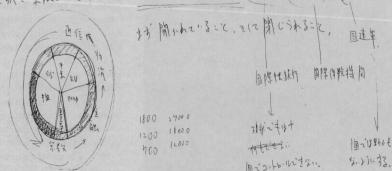

142

概念であり、さらにはある種の価値体系でもある。陸と海とが交差するこの広大な領域ではこれまでいくつもの文明が長きにわたって共存し、混ざり合い、浸透し合ってきたが、同化することも統一されることもなかった。しかし19世紀末から、アジアのすべての地域は植民地化によって西洋的価値観の内面化を経験してきた。内面化された西洋的価値観は、アジアの様々な民族グループによって独自のイデオロギーの力とアイデンティティのシステムへと変換され、それはまたさらに差異や対立、絡み合った関係性を多層的に生み出した。中国の近代史において最も痛ましい経験は日本と深く関わっていて、中国と日本、朝鮮半島、そして台湾との複雑な関係は、戦後も続く冷戦構造の中でのアメリカとの対立とは切っても切れないものだ。近年の中国の急速な台頭に伴うアメリカとの政治的対立やテクノロジー・貿易競争は、近隣諸国に幾度となく緊張をもたらしてきた。政治・安全保障における対立や経済的相互依存の不均衡、歴史の記憶・継承の重なり合い、文化的アイデンティティの混乱——これらはすべて、私たちがアジアの文脈について議論しようとする際にあまりにも多くのパラドックスを生み出す。グローバリゼーションによって増大する貧富の格差、民主主義システムが直面する前例のない危機、いたるところで見られるポピュリズムの台頭などは、素朴な道徳的正義だけでは緊迫する国際政治の問題に対処できないことを示している。既成の理論や概念、およびそれに基づく批評的アプローチではもはや、現実の複雑な課題を有効に理解し説明することはできないのだ。その一方で、互いに依存しながら互いに嫌悪する長年の感情的な関係はさらに悪化の一途を辿っている。

　常に激しく変化し続けるこのアジアという現場では、衝突や危機、災害に反応して私たちはほとんど本能的に行動せざるをえなくなり、物理的体験が速すぎて頭の思考が追いつかなくなる。私たちはみな、アジアを覆って絡み合う緊張の網がますます張り詰めているのを感じていると言っていいだろう。この網はいつか破れるのだろうか？　そのとき私たちに何ができるのだろうか？　加藤翼の作品に登場する、互いに関係し合い、協力し合い、けれど互いに近づくことができないパフォーマーたちの姿を見ていると、ウイルスによって2年間も行動を制限され孤立したあとに人々がどのようにして新たな流れを切り開いていくのか想像がつかない。もちろん私たちを阻むのはウイルスだけではないことを知りながら……。

　私たちが再び会うとき、私たちには抱擁する勇気があるのだろうか？

legacies of historical memories, and the confusion in cultural identity—all leave us with too many paradoxes when we discuss in the context of Asia. The increasing wealth gap brought about by globalization, and the unprecedented crisis faced by the democratic system and the rise of Populism everywhere, make intuitive moral justice seem inadequate to deal with the intensified international political relations. Pre-existing theories and concepts as well as the critical approach based on them, can no longer help us effectively understand or explain complicated realistic topics. All the while, the long-standing emotional relationship of both interdependence and resentment only became more exacerbated than ever.

In the ever drastically changing here and now in Asia, conflicts, crises, and disasters often force us to act almost instinctively, and physical experiences too fast for us to think in time. It is fair to believe that we can all feel the tightening of the intricate net of tension hovering above Asia... Is the net going to break one day? Then what is there for us to do? Seeing how the performers in Tsubasa Kato's works interrelate, collaborate, but can never get close to one another—I find it difficult to imagine how we are going to set into motion again after having been isolated and chained for two years, when we are well aware that the virus is not the only thing that separates us...

Will we be brave enough for an embrace when we meet again?

©Yinlan Lu

王　慰慰（ワン・ウェイウェイ）
香港・CHAT（Centre for Heritage, Arts and Textile）展覧会・コレクションキュレーター。2010年から2017年まで中国・上海当代芸術館（MoCA Shanghai）のキュレーターを務め、2017年には台湾・関渡美術館（Kuandu Museum of Fine Arts）のキュレーター・イン・レジデンス・プログラムと、韓国・国立現代美術館（National Museum of Modern and Contemporary Art）の海外派遣プログラムに参加。その後2018年に第12回上海ビエンナーレの共同キュレーターに任命され、アジアン・カルチュラル・カウンシル香港から個人フェローシップを授与される。2019年から現在まで、東アジアの現代美術に関する研究を行なっている。

Wang Weiwei
The Curator of Exhibitions and Collections at CHAT (Centre for Heritage, Arts and Textile). From 2010 to 2017, Wang was the curator at the Museum of Contemporary Art, Shanghai (MoCA Shanghai).In 2017, She participated at the Curator-in-Residence Programme at the Kuandu Museum of Fine Arts in Taiwan, and the International Researcher Programme at the National Museum of Modern and Contemporary Art in Seoul, South Korea. She was then appointed as the co-curator at the 12th Shanghai Biennale and awarded an Individual Fellowship by Asian Cultural Council Hong Kong in 2018, and since 2019, has conducted on a series of researches on East Asian Contemporary Arts.

加藤 翼

作 家 略 歴

Tsubasa Kato

Biography

1984	埼玉県生まれ
	東京都在住

2015-17	ワシントン大学 建築学部 客員研究員
2010	東京藝術大学 大学院美術研究科絵画専攻油画 修了
2007	武蔵野美術大学 造形学部油絵学科 卒業

個 展

2020	「Superstring Secrets」無人島プロダクション、東京
2018	「40,000km のなかの数メートル【Vietnam ⇄ United States】」無人島プロダクション、東京
2017	「40,000km のなかの数メートル【Mexico City ⇄ Jakarta】」無人島プロダクション、東京
2015	「リーチアウト」無人島プロダクション、東京
2013	「Still the Never-World」無人島プロダクション、東京
2011	「深川、フューチャー、ヒューマニティ」無人島プロダクション／木場公園、東京
	「ホーム、ホテルズ、秀吉、アウェイ」アートエリア B1、大阪

主 な グ ル ー プ 展

2021	「Joy of Singing」オルタナティブスペース ループ、ソウル、韓国
	「Scratching the Surface」ハンブルガー・バーンホフ現代美術館、ベルリン、ドイツ
	「MOMAT コレクション特別編 ニッポンの名作１３０年」東京国立近代美術館、東京
	「横目にみれば」アートギャラリーミヤウチ、広島
	「SOUTH SOUTH TOKYO」タカ・イシイギャラリー、東京
2020	「ギャラリートラック」京都市内
	「UN・TACT」アジア・カルチャー・センター、クァンジュ、韓国
	「2020 年度第 3 期コレクション展」愛知県美術館、愛知
	「Works On Water 2020 Triennial Video Show」Works on Water（オンライン）
	「DOMANI・明日展 plus online 2020：〈前夜〉を生きる」文化庁（オンライン）
	「How Can You Think of Art at a Time Like This?」Art at a Time Like This（オンライン）
	「They Do Not Understand Each Other」大館當代美術館、香港
	「おんらいん大作戦」おんらいん大作戦 Showcase（オンライン）
	「BECOMING A COLLECTIVE BODY」イタリア国立 21 世紀美術館（MAXXI）、ローマ、イタリア
	「Every Man is an Artist - Talking About Artists' Social Engagement」チーウェン・ギャラリー、台北、台湾
2019	「Co/Inspiration in Catastrophes」台北当代芸術館、台北、台湾
	「高松コンテンポラリーアート・アニュアル vol.08 ／社会を解剖する」高松市美術館、香川
	「ご理解いただけましたでしょうか？」インスティトゥット・セルバンテス東京、東京
	「コレクション特集展示 ジャコメッティと Ⅱ」国立国際美術館、大阪
	「サナトリウム」サナトリウム、愛知

Born in 1984, Saitama, Japan
Lives and works in Tokyo

Education

2015-17	Visiting Research Scholar, Department of Architecture, University of Washington, Seattle, USA
2010	M.F.A., Department of Painting, Tokyo University of the Arts, Tokyo, Japan
2007	B.A., Department of Painting, College of Art and Design, Musashino Art University, Tokyo, Japan

Solo Exhibitions

2020	*Superstring Secrets*, MUJIN-TO Production, Tokyo, Japan
2018	*(Drawing) Fractions of the Longest Distance (Vietnam ⇄ United States)*, MUJIN-TO Production, Tokyo, Japan
2017	*(Drawing) Fractions of the Longest Distance (Mexico City ⇄ Jakarta)*, MUJIN-TO Production, Tokyo, Japan
2015	*Reach Out*, MUJIN-TO Production, Tokyo, Japan
2013	*Still the Never-World*, MUJIN-TO Production, Tokyo, Japan
2011	*Fukagawa, Future, Humanity*, MUJIN-TO Production / Kiba Park, Tokyo, Japan
	The Home, Hotels, Hideyoshi, Away, Art Area B1, Osaka, Japan

Selected Group Exhibitions

2021	*Joy of Singing*, Alternative Space Loop, Seoul, South Korea
	Scratching the Surface, Hamburger Bahnhof - Museum für Gegenwart - Berlin, Berlin, Germany
	MOMAT Collection Special: Masterpieces of Japanese Art from the End of the 19th Century to the Present, The National Museum of Modern Art, Tokyo, Japan
	Yokomenimireba, Art Gallery Miyauchi, Hiroshima, Japan
	SOUTH SOUTH TOKYO, Taka Ishii Gallery, Tokyo, Japan
2020	*Gallery Truck*, Kyoto, Japan
	UN・TACT, Asia Culture Center, Gwangju, South Korea
	From the museum collection 2020: third period, Aichi Prefectural Museum of Art, Aichi, Japan
	Works On Water 2020 Triennial Video Show, Works on Water (online)
	DOMANI plus Online 2020: Living on the Eve, Agency for Cultural Affairs (online)
	How Can You Think of Art at a Time Like This? Art at a Time Like This (online)
	They Do Not Understand Each Other, Tai Kwun Contemporary, Hong Kong
	Online Confidential, Online Confidential Showcase (online)
	BECOMING A COLLECTIVE BODY, MAXXI - the National Museum of 21st Century Arts, Rome, Italy
	Every Man is an Artist - Talking About Artists' Social Engagement, Chi-Wen Gallery, Taipei, Taiwan
2019	*Co/Inspiration in Catastrophes*, Museum of Contemporary Art, Taipei, Taiwan
	Takamatsu Contemporary Art Annual Vol.08 / Dissect the Society, Takamatsu Art Museum, Kagawa, Japan

「あいちトリエンナーレ 2019 情の時代」愛知芸術文化センター、愛知

「世界を開くのは誰だ？」豊田市美術館、愛知

「移植」無人島プロダクション、東京

「21st DOMANI: 明日展」国立新美術館、東京

2018 「にんげんレストラン」旧歌舞伎町ブックセンター、東京

「カタストロフと美術のちから」森美術館、東京

「Encounters」PDX コンテンポラリーアート、ポートランド、オレゴン、アメリカ

「コレクション 1：2014 → 1890」国立国際美術館、大阪

「アーツさいたま・きたまちフェスタ Vol. 4・ASK 祭」プラザノースノースギャラリー、埼玉

「out in the cold」ウォーリック・アーツ・センター、コヴェントリー、イギリス

2017 「歴史を体で書く」国立現代美術館、クァチョン、韓国

「Mni Wiconi Summer Festival」シッティング・ブル・カレッジ・ビジターズ・センター、
フォートイェーツ、ノースダコタ、アメリカ

「JWA Video Program」ジョン・ワードル・アーキテクツ、コリングウッド、オーストラリア

「TARO 賞 20年／20人の鬼子たち」岡本太郎記念館、東京

「Condition Report: The Mashup Syndicate」グダン・サリナ・エコシステム、ジャカルタ、
インドネシア

2016 「Regards Croisés / La Fabrique du Regard」ル・バル、パリ、フランス

「Uprisings」ジュ・ド・ポーム国立美術館、パリ、フランス

（「Uprisings」カタルーニャ国立美術館、バルセロナ、スペイン／「Uprisings」トレス・デ・フェブレロ国
立大学美術館、ブエノスアイレス、アルゼンチン／「Levantes」SESC、サンパウロ、ブラジル／
「Sublevaciones」メキシコ国立自治大学現代美術館、メキシコシティ、メキシコ／「Uprisings」ケベック
大学モントリオール校美術館／シネマテーク・ケベコワーズ、モントリオール、カナダへ巡回）

「蜘蛛の糸」豊田市美術館、愛知

「EDITIONS++」無人島プロダクション、東京

「New Colony / Island 2」アートエリア B1、大阪

「East Asian Video Frames: Shades of Urbanization」ポリ美術館、ポリ、フィンランド

2015 「DAM Projects Sunday School #12 - Letter From Tokyo」A_スペース、ロンドン、イギリス

「TSUSHIMA ART FANTASIA in BUSAN」B.C. センター、プサン、韓国

「GERAKAN SENI 2015 ART ON THE MOVE」SMK バンダルバル・スントゥル、クアラルン
プール、マレーシア

「他人の時間」国立国際美術館、大阪

「対馬アートファンタジア 広島ー対馬」泉美術館、広島

「being MAPHILINDO」サバ・アート・ギャラー、コタキナバル、マレーシア

「アーツさいたま・きたまちフェスタ」さいたま市プラザノース 2F ギャラリー、埼玉

「黄金町通路：再訪」高架下スタジオ Site-A ギャラリー、神奈川

「Come Close: Japanese Artists Within their Communities」バス・プロジェクツ、コリング
ウッド、オーストラリア

2014 「二子玉川ビエンナーレ 2014」二子玉川ライズ、東京

「Tokyo Designer's Week 2014 Asia Awards（ヤングクリエイター展）」明治神宮外苑絵画館前、東京

「レッドブル・ミュージック・アカデミー東京 2014」レッドブル・ミュージック・アカデミー、東京

「対馬アートファンタジア」対馬、長崎

「無人島∞」無人島プロダクション、東京

2013 「さっぽろアートステージ」札幌駅前通地下歩行空間、北海道

「二子玉川アートデポ」二子玉川ライズ、東京

「Now Japan; Exhibition with 37 contemporary Japanese artists」クンストハル KAdE、
アメルスフォールト、オランダ

「SNIFF OUT 2013」インテックス大阪、大阪

「玉川上水の件 /Case01.Tamagawa-josui」22:00 画廊、東京

「アートがあればII ー 9人のコレクターによる個人コレクションの場合」東京オペラシティ
アートギャラリー、東京

Falta algo (Something is missing), Instituto Cervantes de Tokio,
Tokyo, Japan

NMAO collection with Alberto Giacometti II, The National
Museum of Art, Osaka, Japan

Sanatorium, Sanatorium, Aichi, Japan

Aichi Triennale 2019: Taming Y/Our Passion, Aichi Arts Center,
Aichi, Japan

Who Opens Up the World? Toyota Municipal Museum of Art,
Aichi, Japan

Transplant, MUJIN-TO Production, Tokyo, Japan

21ST DOMANI: The Art of Tomorrow, The National Art Center,
Tokyo, Japan

2018 NINGEN Restaurant, Former Kabuki-cho Book Center,
Tokyo, Japan

Catastrophe and the Power of Art, Mori Art Museum,
Tokyo, Japan

Encounters, PDX Contemporary Art, Portland, Oregon, USA

Retrospective of the museum collection: 2014 - 1890, The
National Museum of Art, Osaka, Japan

Arts Saitama Kitamachi Fest Vol.4, PLAZA NORTH North
Gallery, Saitama, Japan

out in the cold, Warwick Arts Centre, Coventry, UK

2017 Reenacting history_ Collective Actions and Everyday
Gestures, National Museum of Modern and Contemporary Art,
Gwacheon, South Korea

Mni Wiconi Summer Festival, Sitting Bull College Visitors Center,
Fort Yates, North Dakota, USA

JWA Video Program, John Wardle Architects, Collingwood,
Australia

Twenty Year's of the TARO Award / Twenty Enfants Terrible,
Taro Okamoto Memorial Museum, Tokyo, Japan

Condition Report: The Mashup Syndicate, Gudang Sarinah
Ekosistem, Jakarta, Indonesia

2016 Regards Croisés / La Fabrique du Regard, LE BAL, Paris, France

Uprisings, Jeu de Paume, Paris, France

[traveled to Uprisings, National Art Museum of Catalonia,
Barcelona, Spain / Uprisings, Museum of The National University
of Tres de Febrero, Buenos Aires, Argentina / Levantes, SESC, Saõ
Paulo, Brazil / Sublevaciones, Museo Universitario Arte
Contemporáneo, Mexico City, Mexico / Uprisings, Galerie de
l'UQAM (Université du Québec à Montréal) and Cinémathèque
québécoise, Montréal, Canada]

Spider's Thread – Spinning images of Japanese beauty, Toyota
Municipal Museum of Art, Aichi, Japan

EDITIONS++, MUJIN-TO Production, Tokyo, Japan

New Colony / Island 2, Art Area B1, Osaka, Japan

East Asian Video Frames: Shades of Urbanization, Pori Art
Museum, Pori, Finland

2015 DAM Projects Sunday School #12 - Letter From Tokyo, A_Space,
London, UK

TSUSHIMA ART FANTASIA in BUSAN, B.C.Center, Busan,
South Korea

GERAKAN SENI 2015 ART ON THE MOVE, SMK Bandar Baru
Sentul, Kuala Lumpur, Malaysia

Time of Others, The National Museum of Art, Osaka, Japan

TSUSHIMA ART FANTASIA Hiroshima-Tsushima, Izumi Museum
of Art, Hiroshima, Japan

being MAPHILINDO, Sabah Art Gallery, Kota Kinabalu, Malaysia

Arts Saitama Kitamachi Fest, Saitama Plaza North Gallery,
Saitama, Japan

Passage of KOGANECHO: Revisit, Site A-gallery, Kanagawa,
Japan

Come Close: Japanese Artists Within their Communities, Bus
Projects, Collingwood, Victoria, Australia

2014 Futakotamagawa Biennale 2014, Futakotamagawa Rise, Tokyo, Japan

「Rockaway Call for Ideas ¦ EXPO 1: New York」MoMA PS1 VW ドーム 2、ニューヨーク、アメリカ
「日経アートプロジェクト：アートで遊ぼう！」スペースニオ、東京

2012 「TERATOTERA 祭り 2012」井の頭恩賜公園／吉祥寺バウスシアター、東京
「3・11とアーティスト：進行形の記録」水戸芸術館現代美術ギャラリー、茨城
「Project Daejeon 2012: Energy」テジョン美術館、テジョン、韓国
「Daikanyama Art Street」代官山ヒルサイドテラス、東京
「ヒロシマオーヒロシマフクシマ」旧日本銀行広島支店、広島

2011 「Big in Japan」パディントン・タウン・ホール、シドニー／サウザンズ・ボンド・ベンド、メルボルン、オーストラリア
「黄金町バザール」黄金町エリア、神奈川
「おおさかカンヴァス」大阪市中央公会堂前／大阪城公園／万博記念公園、大阪

2010 「NEO NEW WAVE」island ATRIUM、千葉
「甑島で、つくる。KOSHIKI ART EXHIBITION 2010」上甑島旧港、鹿児島
「六本木クロッシング 2010 展：芸術は可能か？」森美術館、東京
「第 13 回 岡本太郎現代芸術展」川崎市岡本太郎美術館、神奈川

2009 「アートラインかしわ」柏駅前歩行者天国、千葉
「閼（ナントカエイト）」木場公園／旧坂本小学校、東京
「越後妻有アートトリエンナーレ 2009（克雪ダイナモアートプロジェクト）」旧仙田小学校、新潟
「ナント・ビエンナーレ ESTUAIRE 2009（ナントカエイト）」サン＝ナゼール／ナント、フランス
「FRESH EXPAND」URBAN BACK-SIDE LABORATORY R2、千葉
「no name」ZAIM、神奈川／旧立誠小学校、京都
「GEISAI #12」東京ビッグサイト 東 1 ホール、東京

2008 「町に僕たちは必要ですか」上野恩賜公園、東京

主なプロジェクト

2017 「Guerrilla Waves」テン・カフェ、フエ、ベトナム
2015 「Magnetic Tea Party」マリア・エンリケタ・カマリロ・ストリート、メキシコシティ、メキシコ
2013 「Mitakuye Oyasin」ユナイテッド・トライブス・テクニカル・カレッジ、ビスマーク／スー族スタンディングロック居留地、ノースダコタ、アメリカ
「Abandon」デザート・ショアーズ、カリフォルニア、アメリカ
2011 「11.3 PROJECT」いわき市平豊間地区、福島

受 賞 歴

2014 「Tokyo Designer's Week 2014 Asia Awards」企業賞（株式会社 CHINTAI 賞）
2010 「六本木クロッシング 2010 展：芸術は可能か？」特別賞（隈研吾選）
「第 13 回 岡本太郎現代芸術賞」入賞
2009 「GEISAI#12」銅賞、審査員賞（坂田和實賞）

Tokyo Designer's Week 2014 Asia Awards (Young Creator Exhibition), Meiji Jingu Gaien Mae, Tokyo, Japan
Red Bull Music Academy, Red Bull Japan, Tokyo, Japan
TSUSHIMA ART FANTASIA, Tsushima Island, Nagasaki, Japan
MUJIN-TO infinity, MUJIN-TO Production, Tokyo, Japan

2013 *Sapporo Art Stage: Art Street*, Sapporo Ekimae-dori Underground Pedestrian Space, Hokkaido, Japan
FUTAKOTAMAGAWA ART DEPOT, Futakotamagawa Rise, Tokyo, Japan
Now Japan; Exhibition with 37 contemporary Japanese artists, Kunsthal KAdE, Amersfoort, The Netherlands
SNIFF OUT 2013, Intex Osaka, Osaka, Japan
Case01.Tamagawa-josui, 22:00 Gallery, Tokyo, Japan
Why not live for Art? II – 9 collectors reveal their treasures, Tokyo Opera City Art Gallery, Tokyo, Japan
Rockaway Call for Ideas | EXPO 1: New York, MoMA PS1 VW Dome2, New York, USA
Nikkei Art Project, Space Nio Art Gallery, Tokyo, Japan

2012 *TERATOTERA Festival*, Inokashira Park / Baus Theater, Tokyo, Japan
Artists and the Disaster –Documentation in Progress-, Contemporary Art Gallery, Art Tower Mito, Ibaraki, Japan
Project Daejeon 2012: Energy, Daejeon Museum of Art, Daejeon, South Korea
Daikanyama Art Street, Hillside Terrace, Tokyo, Japan
Hiroshima-O Hiroshima Fukushima, The former Bank of Japan Hiroshima branch, Hiroshima, Japan

2011 *Big in Japan*, Paddington Town Hall, Sydney / 1000 £ Bend, Melbourne, Australia
Koganecho Bazaar, Koganecho area, Kanagawa, Japan
Osaka Canvas Project, Osaka City Central Public Hall / Osaka Castle Park / The Expo '70 Commemorative Park, Osaka, Japan

2010 *NEO NEW WAVE*, Island ATRIUM, Chiba, Japan
KOSHIKI ART EXHIBITION 2010, Former port of Kamikoshiki Island, Kagoshima, Japan
Roppongi Crossing 2010: Can There Be Art? Mori Art Museum, Tokyo, Japan
The 13th Exhibition of the Taro Okamoto Award for Contemporary Art, Taro Okamoto Museum of Art, Kawasaki, Kanagawa, Japan

2009 *Art Line Kashiwa*, Front street of Kashiwa Station, Chiba, Japan
ETSU (NANTES CAS 8), Kiba Park / Former Sakamoto elementary school, Tokyo, Japan
Echigo-tsumari Art Triennale (Conquering Snow Dynamo Art Project), Former Senda elementary school, Niigata, Japan
Nantes Biennale ESTUAIRE 2009 (NANTES CAS 8), Saint-Nazaire / Nantes, France
FRESH EXPAND, URBAN BACK-SIDE LABORATORY R2, Chiba, Japan
no name, ZAIM, Kanagawa / Former Rissei elementary school, Kyoto, Japan
GEISAI#12, Tokyo Big Sight, Tokyo, Japan

2008 *Does the Town Need Us?* Ueno Park, Tokyo, Japan

Selected Projects
2017 *Guerrilla Waves*, Then Cafe, Hue, Vietnam
2015 *Magnetic Tea Party*, Maria Enriqueta Camarillo St, Mexico City, Mexico
2013 *Mitakuye Oyasin*, United Tribes Technical College, Bismarck / Standing Rock Sioux Reservation, North Dakota, USA
Abandon, Desert Shores, California, USA
2011 *11.3 PROJECT*, Toyoma district of Iwaki city, Fukushima, Japan

フェローシップ／レジデンシー

2018 「Làng Art Dorm」フエ、ベトナム
2016 「End of Summer」イェール・ユニオン、ポートランド、オレゴン、アメリカ
2015-17 「平成26年度文化庁新進芸術家海外研修制度研修員」シアトル、ワシントン、アメリカ
2015 「日米友好基金 日米芸術家交換プログラム」

会場デザイン（コミッション）

2015 「Don't Follow the Wind / Non-visitor Center」カウンターデザイン、ワタリウム美術館、東京
2012 「サーチプロジェクト vol.1.5」アートエリアB1、大阪

パブリックコレクション（※五十音順）

愛知県美術館
国立国際美術館（大阪）
東京国立近代美術館
豊田市美術館（愛知）
森美術館（東京）
ウルサン美術館（韓国）

パブリケーション

2014 ドキュメンタリー映画「ミタケオヤシン」（監督：江藤孝治）
　　　カタログ『ミタケオヤシン』（出版：グループ現代）
2011 映像記録集 DVD「LOST HOME EMBANKMENT」（制作：加藤翼・無人島プロダクション）
　　　カタログ『加藤翼：ホーム．ホテルズ．秀吉．アウェイ』（出版：アートエリアB1）

Awards

2014 Corporate Award (CHINTAI Corporation Award) - *Tokyo Designers Week 2014 Asia Awards*, Tokyo, Japan
2010 Jury Prize (Kuma Kengo Prize) - *Roppongi Crossing 2010: Can There Be Art?* Tokyo, Japan
　　　Shortlisted - *The 13th Taro Okamoto Award for Contemporary Art*, Kawasaki, Kanagawa, Japan
2009 Bronze Prize and Jury Prize (Sakata Kazumi Prize) - *GEISAI#12*, Tokyo, Japan

Fellowships / Residency

2018 Làng Art Dorm, Hue, Vietnam
2016 End of Summer, Yale Union, Portland, Oregon, USA
2015-17 Program of Overseas Study for Upcoming Artists, supported by Agency for Cultural Affairs Japan
2015 Japan-U.S. Exchange Friendship Program in the Arts, supported by Japan-U.S. Friendship Commission

Commissioned Venue Design

2015 Direction for a visitor counter in *Don't Follow the Wind / Non-visitor Center* exhibition at The Watari Museum of Contemporary Art, Tokyo, Japan
2012 Supervision in *Search Project vol.1.5 project* at Art Area B1, Osaka, Japan

Public Collections

Aichi Prefectural Museum of Art (Japan)
Mori Art Museum (Japan)
The National Museum of Art, Osaka (Japan)
The National Museum of Modern Art, Tokyo (Japan)
Toyota Municipal Museum of Art (Japan)
Ulsan Museum of Art (South Korea)

Publications

2014 [Documentary film] Mitakuye Oyasin (directed by Takaharu Eto)
　　　[Catalogue] Mitakuye Oyasin (published by Group Gendai)
2011 [DVD] LOST HOME EMBANKMENT (produced by Tsubasa Kato and MUJIN-TO Production)
　　　[Catalogue] TSUBASA KATO - THE HOME, HOTELS, HIDEYOSHI, AWAY (published by Art Area B1)

作品リスト　　List of Works

[凡例] 以下の作品リストは2021年7月17日から9月20日まで東京オペラシティアートギャラリーで開催された展覧会「加藤翼 縄張りと島」の出品作品一覧をもとに制作した。●作品情報は、初出のページ番号、作品タイトル、制作年、素材、サイズ（高さ×幅×奥行きcm）、映像作品は尺、撮影者の順に記した。●掲載作品のうち、本書にのみ掲載されている作品については作品名の後にアスタリスク（*）を付した。

[Notes] The following list is based on the list of the exhibited works at the exhibition: *Tsubasa Kato: Turf and Perimeter* which was held at Tokyo Opera City Art Gallery from July 17 to September 20, 2021. ●Information on the works is provided in the following order: page number of the first appearance, title of work, year of production, material, size (H × W × D in cm) or the length of videos, and the photograph/film credit. ●Works marked with asterisks (*) appear only in this book.

p. 3
g.g.g. (grand all, ground, gladiator) **02**
2007
映像（32秒）
Video (0′32″)

p. 4
The Lighthouses - 11.3 PROJECT
2011
映像（6分25秒）
Video (6′25″)

p. 5
Abandon (Black Hills)*
2013
ラムダプリント
Lambda print
46.0 × 69.0 cm

Boarding School
2013
映像（1分21秒）
Video (1′21″)

Boarding School (Process)
2013
映像（2分37秒）
Video (2′37″)

Black Snake
2017
映像（40秒、撮影：平野由香里）
Video (0′40″/ filmed by Yukari Hirano)

p. 6
Underground Orchestra
2017
映像（5分38秒）
Video (5′38″)

Woodstock 2017
2017
映像（4分7秒、演奏：デンタルの唾）
Video (4′07″/ performed by Dentaru No Tsuba)

p. 7
2679
2019
映像（4分15秒、演奏：摩耶・無我・モーラン、高橋ルーク、巴山剛、撮影：青石太郎、平野由香里）
Video (4′15″/ performed by Maya Muga Moeran, Luke Takahashi, and Tsuyoshi Tomoyama / filmed by Taro Aoishi, Yukari Hirano)

Guerrilla Waves
2017
映像（5分57秒）
Video (5′57″)

Break it Before it's Broken
2015
映像（4分49秒、撮影：青石太郎）
Video (4′49″/ filmed by Taro Aoishi)

p. 8
言葉が通じない
They Do Not Understand Each Other
2014
映像（5分14秒）／ラムダプリント（撮影：坂倉圭一）
Video (5′14″) / Lambda print (photographed by Keiichi Sakakura)
35.0 × 70.0 cm

Superstring Secrets: Hong Kong
2020
映像（3面7分41秒、翻訳：楊天帥）
Three videos (7′41″/ translated by Tinshui Yeung)

Superstring Secrets: Tokyo
2020
映像（3面10分23秒、撮影：青石太郎、翻訳：ライアン・ホームバーグ）
Three videos (10′23″/ filmed by Taro Aoishi / translated by Ryan Holmberg)

p. 24
Abandon (Grand Canyon)*
2013
ラムダプリント
Lambda print
46.0 × 69.0 cm

p. 25
Abandon (South Dakota)*
2013
ラムダプリント
Lambda print
35.0 × 70.0 cm

Abandon (Monument Valley)*
2013
ラムダプリント
Lambda print
35.0 × 70.0 cm

p. 29
Abandon (Devils Tower)
2013
ラムダプリント
Lambda print
46.0 × 69.0 cm

p. 36
H.H.H.A. （ホーム，ホテルズ，秀吉，アウェイ）**03**
H.H.H.A. (The Home, Hotels, Hideyoshi, Away) 03
2011
映像（2分56秒）
Video (2′56″)

p. 41
Superstring Secrets: Hong Kong – Tai Wo*
2020
ラムダプリント
Lambda print
29.0 × 43.5 cm

Superstring Secrets: Hong Kong – Fo Tan*
2020
ラムダプリント
Lambda print
29.0 × 43.5 cm

p. 44
Can You Hear Me?
2015
映像（4面同期3分22秒、Gigarunt として）
Four synchronized videos (3′22″/ as Gigarunt)
31.5 × 62.0 × 31.5 cm

p. 48
Listen to the Same Wall
2015
映像（3面同期10分8秒）
Three synchronized videos (10′8″)

p. 51
凹凸 **01** (Concave-Convex 01)
2007
映像（3分24秒、撮影：平野由香里）
Video (3′24″/ filmed by Yukari Hirano)

g.g.g. (1 / 12.5)
2007
模型
Wooden model
37.0 × 40.5 × 50.5 cm

p. 52
ドローイング（g.g.g.）
Drawing (g.g.g.)
2007
水彩
Watercolor on paper
21.0 × 30.0 cm

p. 53
g.g.g. (1 / 2.5)
2007
構造体
Wooden structure
182.0 × 201.0 × 250.0 cm

p. 56
Turningman
2012/2021
映像、構造体、ロープ、ライブカメラ
Video, wooden structure, rope, and monitoring camera
555.0 × 371.5 × 296.0 cm

Turningman
2012
ラムダプリント
Lambda print
61.4 × 92.1 cm

p. 58
凹凸 **02** (Concave-Convex 02)
2008
映像（2分42秒、撮影：平野由香里）
Video (2′42″/ filmed by Yukari Hirano)

p. 63
The Raft of _____*
2016
映像（3分39秒、撮影：マット・ジェイ）
Video (3′39″/ filmed by Matt Jay)

Pass Between Magnetic Tea Party*
2015
テーブルクロス、木パネル
Tablecloths on wooden panels
270.0 × 180.0 × 939.0 cm

p. 66
ISEYA Calling
2012
映像（3分01秒）
Video (3′01″)

p. 68
Abandon (Salton Sea)
2013
映像（2分48秒、撮影：平野由香里）
Video (2′48″/ filmed by Yukari Hirano)

p. 72
F.F.H. (1 / 12.5)
2011
模型

Wooden model
17.9 × 47.0 × 53.6 cm
個人蔵 / Private collection

p. 74
Haul the Whale First
2008
映像（3分17秒／映像提供：『僕らのカヌーができるまで』）
Video (3´17˝/ footage courtesy of "Bokura-no Canoe-ga
Dekirumade")

p. 78
第十八回オリンピック東京大会
XVIII OLYMPIAD TOKYO 1964
2021
本、ミニチュアフィギュア、メトロノーム、ロープ
Book, miniature figures, metronome, and ropes
23.0 × 37.5 × 26.5 cm

城と茶室
The Japanese Castle and Teahouse
2021
本、ミニチュアフィギュア、マッチ箱、ロープ
Book, miniature figures, match box, and ropes
17.5 × 37.0 × 27.0 cm

p. 80
法隆寺と斑鳩の寺
Horyuji Temple and Other Temples in Ikaruga
2021
本、ミニチュアフィギュア、ガルーダ木彫、ロープ
Book, miniature figures, Garuda wood carving, and ropes
19.5 × 37.0 × 27.0 cm

p. 82
LES TROIS GRANDES EGYPTIENNES
2021
本、ミニチュアフィギュア、ソーラーパネル、ロープ
Book, miniature figures, solar panel, and ropes
20.0 × 29.5 × 29.5 cm

2001 WORLD CALLIGRAPHY BIENNALE
OF JEOLLABUK-DO 3rd
2021
本、ミニチュアフィギュア、磁石、ロープ
Book, miniature figures, magnet, and ropes
13.0 × 33.5 × 26.0 cm

日本列島重力異常図（東京）
GRAVITY ANOMALY MAP AND AROUND THE JAPANESE ISLANDS : Tokyo
2021
2色フィルム、ガラス、ミニチュアフィギュア、温度計、ロープ
Two-colour transparent films, glass plate, miniature figures,
thermometer, and ropes
14.0 × 39.8 × 39.8 cm

FAR OUT
2021
本、ミニチュアフィギュア、仏像のレプリカ、ロープ
Book, miniature figures, replica of Wooden Buddha
statue, and ropes
22.0 × 30.0 × 30.0 cm

p. 83
日本列島重力異常図（対馬）
GRAVITY ANOMALY MAP AND AROUND THE JAPANESE ISLANDS : Tsushima island
2021
2色フィルム、ガラス、ミニチュアフィギュア、釣り針、ロープ
Two-colour transparent films, glass plate, miniature figures,
fishhook, and ropes
10.0 × 39.8 × 39.8 cm

p. 84
日本列島重力異常図（福島）
GRAVITY ANOMALY MAP AND AROUND THE JAPANESE ISLANDS : Fukushima
2021
2色フィルム、ガラス、ミニチュアフィギュア、ガイガーカ
ウンター、ロープ
Two-colour transparent films, glass plate, miniature figures,
geiger counter, and ropes
12.0 × 39.8 × 39.8 cm

INTRODUCING JAPAN
2021
本、ミニチュアフィギュア、マイクロメーター、金属片、ロープ
Book, miniature figures, micrometer, metal, and ropes
24.5 × 30.4 × 23.0 cm

p. 85
人体絵本
INSIDE THE BODY
2021
本、ミニチュアフィギュア、顕微鏡、ロープ
Book, miniature figures, microscope, and ropes
22.5 × 36.0 × 27.0 cm

世界大地図帳
GRAND ATRAS WORLD
2021
本、ミニチュアフィギュア、スピーカー、ロープ
Book, miniature figures, speaker, and ropes
13.0 × 43.5 × 30.0 cm

p. 86
Tepee Rocket*
2013
映像（2面同期1分24秒）
Two synchronized videos (1´24˝)

p. 93
H.H.H.A.（ホーム，ホテルズ，秀吉，アウェイ）02*
H.H.H.A. (The Home, Hotels, Hideyoshi, Away)02
2011
映像（3分00秒）
Video (3´00˝)

p. 94
H.H.H.H.（ホーム，ホテルズ，ハルニャン，ハウス）
H.H.H.H. (The home, hotels, Harnyan, the house)
2008
映像（19秒）
Video (0´19˝)

p. 105
I 🖤 see you
2015
映像（2面同期8分55秒、撮影：青石太郎）
Two synchronized videos (8´55˝/ filmed by Taro Aoishi)

p. 109
Superstring Secrets: Hong Kong – Hang Hau*
2020
ラムダプリント
Lambda print
29.0 × 43.5 cm

p. 112
Superstring Secrets: Tokyo – Olympic Stadium
2020
ラムダプリント
Lambda print
29.0 × 43.5 cm

Superstring Secrets: Tokyo – Tokyo Metropolitan Gymnasium*
2020
ラムダプリント
Lambda print
29.0 × 43.5 cm

p. 118
Superstring Secrets: Tokyo – Ariake Tennis Park*
2020
ラムダプリント
Lambda print
29.0 × 43.5 cm

p. 124
F.F.H.（深川，フューチャー，ヒューマニティ）
F.F.H. (Fukagawa, Future, Humanity)
2011
映像（3面同期4分3秒）
Three synchronized videos (4´03˝)

p. 133
NATIONAL GEOGRAPHIC SATELLITE ATLAS
OF THE WORLD
2021
本、ミニチュアフィギュア、水筒、ロープ
Book, miniature figures, water bottle, and ropes
18.0 × 36.0 × 27.0 cm

p. 134
Superstring Secrets: Tokyo – Odaiba Marine Park
2020
ラムダプリント
Lambda print
29.0 × 43.5 cm

展覧会にのみ出品された作品

凹凸 04 (Concave-Convex 04)
2008
映像（1分28秒、撮影：エドワード・ケン・フォックス）
Video (1´28˝/ filmed by Edward Ken Fox)

A
2009
映像（3秒、撮影：西岳拡貴）
Video (0´03˝/ filmed by Hiroki Nishitake)

Closing a Bird's Barn
2009
映像（52秒、撮影：坂口直也）
Video (0´52˝/ filmed by Naoya Sakaguchi)

ドローイング（Brother LEO）
Drawing (Brother LEO)
2010

Model 06: China The Great in Hong Kong
2020
本、ミニチュアフィギュア、兵馬俑のレプリカ、ロープ
Book, miniature figures, replica of Terracotta
Warriors, and ropes
24.0 × 53.0 × 32.0 cm
塩入敏治氏蔵 / collection of Mr. Toshiharu Shioiri

Superstring Secrets: Hong Kong – Tai Po
2020
ラムダプリント
Lambda print
29.0 × 43.5 cm

STRANGE AMAZING
AND MYSTERIOUS PLACES
2021
本、ミニチュアフィギュア、木製墨壺、ロープ
Book, miniature figures, carpenter's ink pot, and ropes
21.0 × 36.0 × 26.0 cm

One Digital Day
2021
本、ミニチュアフィギュア、上皿はかり、ロープ
Book, miniature figures, scale, and ropes
23.0 × 36.5 × 25.5 cm

The Best of LIFE
2021
本、ミニチュアフィギュア、ルーペ、ロープ
Book, miniature figures, loupe, and ropes
14.0 × 33.5 × 27.0 cm

20世紀全記録
Chronik 1900-1986
2021
本、ミニチュアフィギュア、メトロノーム、ロープ
Book, miniature figures, metronome, and ropes
49.5 × 34.5 × 7.0 cm

謝　辞

本書の出版にあたり多大なご協力
を賜りました下記の各位、機関、
ならびに、ここにお名前を記すこ
とのできなかった数多くの関係者、
協力者のみなさまに深く感謝申し
あげます。（順不同・敬称略）

Acknowledgements

We would like to express our sincere
gratitude to all the following and all
those whose names are not mentioned
here for their generous assistance,
support and contributions to this
publication.

Angry Ai	Angry Ai
毒山　凡太朗	Bontaro Dokuyama
江藤　孝治	Takaharu Eto
株式会社　不二榮	Fujiei Corporation
藤城　里香	Rika Fujiki
藤村　祥馬	Shoma Fujimura
藤生　恭平	Kyohei Fujio
福島　周平	Shuhei Fukushima
福田　周平	Shuhei Fukuda
株式会社　グループ現代	Group Gendai Films Co., Ltd.
原　淳之介	Junnosuke Hara
畠山　祐介	Yusuke Hatakeyama
平野　由香里	Yukari Hirano
市村　隼人	Hayato Ichimura
甲斐　宣明	Semmei Kai
柿内　由希子	Yukiko Kakiuchi
加茂　昴	Akira Kamo
寛太郎工務店	Kantaro Komuten
川田　淳	Jun Kawada
岸本　望	Nozomu Kishimoto
北川　陽史	Yoji Kitagawa
森山　泰地	Taichi Moriyama
無人島プロダクション	MUJIN-TO Production
村山　悟郎	Goro Murayama
牟田口　景	Hikari Mutaguchi
有限会社　六文舎	Rokumonsha
坂倉　弘祐	Kosuke Sakakura
作田　知樹	Tomoki Sakuta
佐藤　洋平	Yohei Sato
柴田　恵子	Keiko Shibata
塩入　敏治	Toshiharu Shioiri
Sous Chef	Sous Chef
須賀　悠介	Yusuke Suga
和田　晋侍	Shinji Wada
若栗　真由美	Mayumi Wakaguri
ジェレミー・ウールズィー	Jeremy Woolsey
YANTOR	YANTOR
吉野　誠一	Seiichi Yoshino

写真クレジット：
垂水佳菜（p. 2）、坂口直也（p. 10）、平野由香里（pp. 10, 13-15, 26-27, 32-33, 40, 46-47, 86-87, 98-99, 106）、エドワード・ケン・
フォックス（pp. 14-15, 150）、BARBARA DARLINg（pp. 14-15）、宮島径（pp. 16-17）、森田兼次（pp. 44, 63, 114-117, 120）、坂倉
圭一（p.50）佐藤洋平（pp.73, 76-78）、グループ現代（画像提供／pp. 88-89）、青石太郎（pp. 95-97）、Srap Dsign（pp. 96-97, 102-
103, 104, 121）、Lucien Ng（p.119）、弘瀬みどり（p.120）

Photograph credits：
Kana Tarumi (p. 2), Naoya Sakaguchi (p. 10), Yukari Hirano (pp. 10, 13-15, 26-27, 32-33, 40, 46-47, 86-87, 98-99, 106), Edward Ken Fox (pp. 14-15, 150),
BARBARA DARLINg (pp. 14-15), Kei Miyajima (pp. 16-17), Kenji Morita (pp. 44, 63, 114-117, 120), Keiichi Sakakura (p. 50), Yohei Sato (pp. 73, 76-78),
Courtesy of Group Gendai (pp. 88-89), Taro Aoishi (pp. 95-97), Srap Dsign (pp. 96-97, 102-103, 104, 121), Lucien Ng (p. 119), Midori Hirose (p. 120)

本書は下記の展覧会に際して出版されました。

［展覧会］
加藤翼　縄張りと島
会期：2021 年 7 月 17 日〜9 月 20 日
会場：東京オペラシティ アートギャラリー
主催：公益財団法人 東京オペラシティ文化財団
協賛：NTT 都市開発株式会社
協力：無人島プロダクション／福徳産業株式会社／ARTISTS' GUILD ／ WHITELIGHT

縄張りと島
Turf and Perimeter

加藤 翼
Tsubasa Kato

2021 年 9 月 20 日　初版第 1 刷発行

著者：加藤 翼
執筆：堀 元彰、王 慰慰
対談：ケン・タダシ・オオシマ、関野吉晴
翻訳：ライアン・ホームバーグ（和文英訳／pp. 3-8, 9-65, 73-121）、三田野乃花（英文和訳／
pp. 9-65, 137-143）、リンジー・サン（中文英訳／pp. 137-143）
写真（展示風景）：森田兼次
ブックデザイン：吉岡秀典（セプテンバーカウボーイ）
編集：綾女欣伸（朝日出版社）、仁科えい（朝日出版社）
編集協力：平野由香里、堀 元彰（東京オペラシティ アートギャラリー）、
瀧上 華（東京オペラシティ アートギャラリー）、無人島プロダクション

発行者：原 雅久
発行所：株式会社 朝日出版社
〒101-0065 東京都千代田区西神田 3-3-5
tel. 03-3263-3321/ fax. 03-5226-9599
http://www.asahipress.com/

印刷・製本：株式会社 八紘美術

This book is published for the following exhibition.

[Exhibition]
Tsubasa Kato: Turf and Perimeter
Date: 17 July–20 September, 2021
Venue: Tokyo Opera City Art Gallery
Organizer: Tokyo Opera City Cultural Foundation
Sponsor: NTT Urban Development Corporation
Cooperation: MUJIN-TO Production/ Fukutoku Corporation/
ARTISTS' GUILD/ WHITELIGHT

[Catalogue]
Turf and Perimeter: Tsubasa Kato

First edition published on 20 September, 2021

Author: Tsubasa Kato
Text: Motoaki Hori, Wang Weiwei
Dialogue: Ken Tadashi Oshima, Yoshiharu Sekino
Translation: Ryan Holmberg (Japanese/English: pp. 3-8, 9-65,
73-121), Nonoka Mita (English/Japanese: pp. 9-65, 137-143),
Lindsey Sun (Chinese/English: pp. 137-143)
Photography (Installation View): Kenji Morita
Design: Hidenori Yoshioka (September Cowboy)
Editor: Yoshinobu Ayame (Asahi Press), Ei Nishina (Asahi Press)
Editorial Associates: Yukari Hirano, Motoaki Hori (Tokyo
Opera City Art Gallery), Hana Takigami (Tokyo Opera City Art
Gallery), MUJIN-TO Production

Publisher: Masahisa Hara
Published by Asahi Press Inc.
3-3-5 Nishi-Kanda, Chiyoda-ku, Tokyo 101-0065 Japan
tel.+81-3-3263-3321/ fax.+81-3-5226-9599

Printed by Hakkou Bijyutsu Co., Ltd.